Economic Freedom
of North America

Economic Freedom of North America

Amela Karabegović

Fred McMahon

& Dexter Samida

with
Glen Mitchell & Chris Schlegel

The Fraser Institute
Canada

National Center for Policy Analysis
United States of America

Canadian Publications Mail Sales Product Agreement #0087246
Return postage guaranteed.

Editing and design by Lindsey Thomas Martin
Cover design by Brian Creswick @ GoggleBox

Printed in Canada

National Library of Canada Cataloguing in Publication Data

Karabegović, Amela, 1977–
    Economic freedom of North America / Amela Karabegović, Fred McMahon & Dexter Samida;
    with Glen Mitchell & Chris Schlegel.

    Copublished by: National Center for Policy Analysis.
    Includes bibliographical references.
    ISBN 0-88975-197-8

    1. Free enterprise--Canada.   2. Free enterprise--United States.   3. Canada--Economic conditions--
1991-   4. United States--Economic conditions--2001-   I. Samida, Dexter.   II. McMahon, Fred.
III. Fraser Institute (Vancouver, B.C.)   IV. National Center for Policy Analysis (U.S.)   V. Title.

HC115.K3358 2002   330.971'0648   C2002-911487-X

Table of Contents

Acknowledgments

The Lotte and John Hecht Memorial Foundation and the W. Garfield Weston Foundation have generously supported this research. The authors would also like to acknowledge the assistance of Michael Walker, Steven Easton, Robert Lawson, Faisal Arman, and Joel Emes in developing the methodology and collecting the data. Any remaining errors and omissions are the responsibility of the authors.

About the Authors

Amela Karabegović is a Research Economist at The Fraser Institute. She holds a B.M. (Great Distinction) in General Management from the University of Lethbridge in Alberta, and an M.A. in Economics from the Simon Fraser University in British Columbia.

Fred McMahon is the director of the Centre for Trade Globalization Studies at The Fraser Institute. He is the author of several books including, *Looking the Gift Horse in the Mouth: The Impact of Federal Transfers on Atlantic Canada,* which won the US$10,000 Sir Antony Fisher International Memorial Award for advancing public policy debate. He has consulted on development in South America and been commissioned for research for the United Nations. His columns have appeared in a number of publications including *The Wall Street Journal, Policy Options, National Post, Globe and Mail, Ottawa Citizen, Vancouver Sun,* and *Montreal Gazette.*

Glenn Mitchell is a writer, editor and media consultant in Dallas, Texas, who has worked on a number of projects for the National Center for Policy Analysis. He is the editor of *Notes on Freedom: Individual Liberty vs. Government Tyranny, 18th Century and Today, A Study of Cato's Letters* (Dallas, TX: NCPA, 2000).

Dexter Samida was formerly a Research Economist at The Fraser Institute. He obtained a B. Comm. (high honours) from the University of Saskatchewan and an M.A. in Economics from the University of Toronto in Ontario. His research and writing at The Fraser Institute included work on economic freedom, foreign aid, taxation policy, international trade, globalization, and consumerism. His work has appeared in the *National Post,* the *Globe and Mail* and many regional newspapers. Currently he is studying law at the University of Chicago.

Chris Schlegel, formerly an economist at The Fraser Institute, is employed by the New Hampshire Public Utilities Commission. He worked on this project while at The Fraser Institute.

About the Participating Institutes

Co-publishers of *Economic Freedom of North America*

The Fraser Institute
Canada

The Fraser Institute is an independent Canadian economic and social research and educational organization. It has as its objective the redirection of public attention to the role of competitive markets in providing for the well-being of Canadians. Where markets work, the Institute's interest lies in trying to discover prospects for improvement. Where markets do not work, its interest lies in finding the reasons. Where competitive markets have been replaced by government control, the interest of the Institute lies in documenting objectively the nature of the improvement or deterioration resulting from government intervention.

The work of the Institute is assisted by an Editorial Advisory Board of internationally renowned economists. The Fraser Institute is a national, federally chartered, non-profit organization financed by the sale of its publications and the tax-deductible contributions of its members. (E-mail: info@fraserinstitute.ca; website: http://www.fraserinstitute.ca)

National Center for Policy Analysis
United States of America

The National Center for Policy Analysis (NCPA) is a nonprofit, nonpartisan organization, established in 1983. The NCPA's goal is to develop and promote private alternatives to government regulation and control, solving problems by relying on the strengths of the competitive, entrepreneurial private sector.

The NCPA's motto—Making Ideas Change the World—reflects the belief that ideas have enormous power to change the course of human events. The NCPA seeks to unleash the power of ideas for positive change by identifying, encouraging, and aggressively marketing the best scholarly research.

The NCPA has its headquarters in Dallas, Texas as well as a highly effective office in Washington, DC, that sponsors Capitol Hill briefings, conferences and testimony by NCPA experts before congressional committees. The NCPA serves as a source of "outside-the-Beltway" thinking for Capitol Hill deliberations. (E-mail: ncpa@ncpa.org; website: http://www.ncpa.org)

Economic Freedom
of North America

Executive Summary

Economic freedom has a powerful effect across North America on the prosperity and economic growth of US states and Canadian provinces.

Economic Freedom of North America presents the first comprehensive economic freedom ratings for US states and Canadian provinces. The study rates economic freedom on a 10-point scale for two indexes. An all-government index captures the impact of restrictions on freedom by all levels of government. A subnational index captures the impact of restrictions by state or provincial governments and local governments. *Economic Freedom of North America* employs nine variables in three areas: 1. Size of Government; 2. Takings and Discriminatory Taxation; and 3. Labor Market Freedom.

Not only is economic freedom important for the level of prosperitty, growht in economic freedom spurs economic growth. As expected, the impact of economic freedom at the all-government level is greater than the impact at the subnational level since the first index captures a broader range of limitations on economic freedom than the second.

The econometric testing shows that a one-point improvement on the all-government index increases per-capita GDP by US$7,185 for US states and by US$2,558 (C$3,798) for Canadian provinces. On the subnational index, a one-point improvement increases per-capita GDP by US$3,328 for US states and by US$1,859 (C$2,761) for Canadian provinces.

A one-percentage point improvement on the all-government index increases per-capita economic growth by 1.00% for US states and by 0.52% for Canadian provinces. On the subnational index, a one-percentage point improvement increases per-capita economic growth by 0.48% for US states and by 0.40% for Canadian provinces.

The econometric results are remarkably stable and consistent through a number of sensitivity tests presented in this paper, with more to be found on the website, www.freetheworld.com.

The results show that, while economic freedom has a powerful impact in Canada, its impact on US states is far greater. This is likely because of Canada's fiscal federalism. This system transfers money from rich to poor provinces. Since economic freedom spurs prosperity and growth, fiscal federalism in effect transfers money from relatively free provinces to relatively unfree provinces, muting the impact of economic freedom and perversely creating incentives for provincial politicians to limit economic freedom and, thus, economic growth since this increases the flow of federal transfers, which are directly controlled by these politicians. This enhances their power and their ability to reward friends and penalize enemies.

Generally, US states have been able to realize the gains economic freedom generates while Canadian provinces have lost opportunity due to weak levels of economic freedom and the structure of Canadian federalism.

All provinces, except Alberta, are clustered at the bottom of the rankings of both the all-government and the subnational economic freedom indexes and also have low levels of prosperity. Ontario is the only other province that is freer than some states in some years. Yet, its level of prosperity in 2000 is ahead of only the three poorest states, West Virginia, Mississippi, and Montana, states that also suffer weak economic-freedom scores.

Although exceptions occur, changes in prosperity closely follow changes in economic freedom. Massachusetts is an interesting example. In 1981, the beginning of the period under study, Massachusetts had a low economic-freedom score and an economy that performed below the national average. Massachusetts' economic freedom increased through the 1980s and its economy caught up to the national average. Economic freedom declined in the early 1990s and relative prosperity fell back. Massachusetts' economic freedom again increased from the mid-

1990s onwards and, by 2000, it was tied as the second wealthiest state in the union. Prosperity has also returned to Massachusetts.

In Canada, Alberta followed a similar pattern. Economic freedom and economic activity weakened into the early 1990s. The province then recorded strong gains in economic freedom through the rest of the 1990s. During this period, the province's economic health was restored.

Measuring economic freedom, however, does not capture all influences on economic activity. A few exceptions are found, such as Alaska, which is wealthier than its level of economic freedom would suggest; and Louisiana, which is poorer than its level of freedom would suggest. Factors such as resource wealth, proximity to transportation routes, even a culture of corruption can affect growth rates.

The evolution of economic freedom in North America follows the expected pattern. In the United States, at the all-government level, economic freedom increases through the 1980s, coinciding with the Reagan era. It fell in the early 1990s, following tax increases under the Bush and early Clinton administrations and then begins to rise again. At the subnational level, the pattern is the same but less pronounced. Many states embarked upon Reagan-like government restructuring, but not all, and often not at the same level of intensity, or in the same time frame.

In Canada through the 1980s, economic freedom remained fairly constant at the subnational level while it increased somewhat at the all-government level, perhaps as a result of a change of federal government, and a resulting change in policy, in 1984. In both indexes, economic freedom falls in Canada in the early 1990s and then begins to rise. In early 1990s, Canadian governments began to address debt and deficit problems but more often through increased taxation than through lower spending. As debts and deficits were brought under control, governments began to reduce some tax rates through the mid- and, particularly, late 1990s. Also in this period, fiscally conservative governments were elected in Canada's two richest provinces, Alberta and Ontario.

Overall patterns in Canada and the United States are similar. However, during the late 1980s and early 1990s, Canadian governments relied on taxes to solve the deficit problem more than US governments did. Thus, the gap between Canada and the United States in economic freedom grew through this period, before returning to about its 1981 level in 2000.

Chapter 1: Economic Freedom & the Index

Introduction

The index of the Economic Freedom of North America is an attempt to gauge the extent of the restrictions on economic freedom imposed by governments in North America. This study employs two indexes. The first is the subnational index, which measures the impact of provincial and municipal governments in Canada and state and local governments in the United States. The second index, called the all-government index, includes the impact of all levels of government—federal, provincial/state, and municipal/local—in Canada and the United States. All 10 provinces and 50 states are included in both indexes. Although this study does not rank Mexican states, future research will endeavour to do so.

The study examines the impact of economic freedom on both the level of economic activity and the growth of economic activity. The econometric testing presented in this paper shows that in North America economic freedom fosters prosperity and growth. Economic freedom increases the affluence of individuals. This finding is consistent with other studies of economic freedom.[1] The results are highly significant and remarkably stable through a number of different sensitivity tests.

The majority of US states have high levels of economic freedom and prosperity. Only a handful of states, most notably West Virginia, have consistently low levels of economic freedom. Other states, such as Colorado, Tennessee, Nevada, Indiana, Georgia, Connecticut, Louisiana, and Texas, have consistently high levels of economic freedom. All, with the exception of Louisiana, either exceed the United States' average per-capita GDP or have been exceeding average economic growth in the United States. The states that have consistently low levels of economic freedom—West Virginia, Maine, New Mexico, Arkansas, Alaska, and Rhode Island—either suffer from a GDP that is below the national average or that is declining against the national average.

Some states have dramatically changed their economic freedom rating over the period. Massachusetts went from the bottom five to the top five in all-government rankings over the period. During this period, its economy, which had been under-performing the national average, became one of the three richest states in the United States. Oklahoma fell dramatically in the economic freedom rankings and in relative wealth over the period.

Unfortunately, Canadian provinces are poorly positioned to benefit from economic freedom. With the exception of Alberta and, to a lesser extent, Ontario, they are all clustered at the bottom of the economic freedom ratings and are the poorest jurisdictions in North America. Figures 1 and 2 illustrate economic freedom scores and the large differences between US states and Canadian provinces.

Alberta's economic freedom scores put it roughly in the middle of the pack. It also has a middling level of economic activity within the North American context, hardly the star performer usually visualized in Canada. Ontario has a more typically Canadian score in economic freedom. As for wealth, in 2000, the most recent year for which comprehensive data is available, Ontario places ahead only of the three poorest US states, West Virginia, Mississippi, and Montana. This is a very disappointing result for the province that is normally considered Canada's industrial heartland, though its prosperity ranks far behind advanced, industrial US states.

What is Economic Freedom?

Gwartney et al. defined economic freedom as follows:

> Individuals have economic freedom when (a) property they acquire without the use of force, fraud, or theft is protected from physical invasions by others and (b) they are free to use,

exchange, or give their property as long as their actions do not violate the identical rights of others. Thus, an index of economic freedom should measure the extent to which rightly acquired property is protected and individuals are engaged in voluntary transactions. (1996: 12)

The freest economies operate with a minimal level of government interference, relying upon personal choice and markets to answer the basic economic questions such as what is to be produced, how it is to be produced, how much is produced, and for whom production is intended. As government imposes restrictions on these choices, the level of economic freedom declines.

The research flowing from the data generated by the *Economic Freedom of the World* reports,[2] a project The Fraser Institute initiated almost 20 years ago, shows that economic freedom is important to the well-being of a nation's citizens. This research has found that economic freedom is positively correlated with per-capita income, economic growth, greater life expectancy, lower child mortality, the development of democratic institutions, civil and political freedoms, and other desirable social and economic outcomes. Just as *Economic Freedom of the World* seeks to measure economic freedom on an international basis, *Economic Freedom of North America* has the goal of measuring differences in economic freedom between the Canadian provinces and US states.

This study looks at the 10 Canadian provinces—excluding Yukon, the Northwest Territories, and Nunavut—and the 50 US states from 1981 to 2000. Each province and state is ranked on economic freedom at the subnational and all-government levels. This helps isolate the impact of different levels of government on economic freedom in North America.

In extending the work on economic freedom, it would seem obvious to include the tried and tested measures used in *Economic Freedom of the World*. This is not as easy as it sounds. Some categories of the world index have too little variance among North American jurisdictions to measured accurately. For example, the stability of the legal system (one of the areas used in *Economic Freedom of the World*) does not differ much among states and provinces. Variables such as the private ownership of banks, avoidance of negative interest rates, monetary policy, freedom to own foreign currency, the right to international exchange, structure of capital markets, and black-market exchange rates are ineffective for an inquiry into the state of economic freedom within North America, particularly at a subnational level.

However, economic freedom varies across North America in three important aspects, which we attempt to capture in this index: size of government; takings and discriminatory taxation; and labor market flexibility. A fourth, potentially important, area of difference, restriction on the movement of goods within North America, had to be left out due to lack of data. This may be particularly important in the Canadian context, since Canada retains a number of internal trade barriers.[3]

Data limitations also create difficulties in testing relationships between economic freedom and key economic variables. For example, we are only partly able to construct a growth model. Data on investment for individual states, an important part of any growth model, are not available. Fortunately, as discussed later, the effect of omitting investment variable on the estimated economic freedom coefficient is likely to be of little quantitative significance. High school graduation rates are used as a proxy for human capital but in our testing this variable often does not have the expected sign and is seldom significant in the regressions in which it is included.

Due to data limitations and revisions, some time periods are either not directly comparable or are not available. When necessary we have used the data closest to the missing time period as an estimate for the missing data. If there have been changes in this component during this period, this procedure would introduce some amount of measurement error in the estimate of economic freedom for the particular data point. However, omitting the component in the cases when it is missing and basing the index score on the remaining components may create more bias in the estimate of overall economic freedom.

The *theory* of economic freedom[4] is no different at the subnational and all-government level than it is at the global level, although different proxies consistent with the theory of economic freedom must be found that suit subnational and all-government measures. The nine variables chosen fall into three areas: Size of Government, Takings and Discriminatory Taxation, and Labor Market Freedom. Before we discuss what each area includes, it should be noted that most of the variables we use are calculated as a ratio of gross

Figure 1: Summary of 2000 Ratings—All-Government

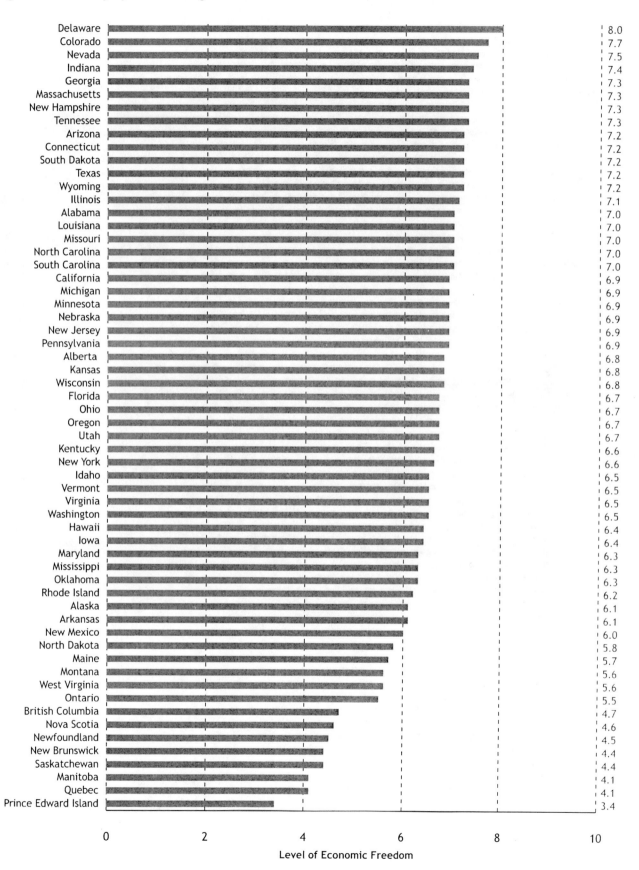

State/Province	Rating
Delaware	8.0
Colorado	7.7
Nevada	7.5
Indiana	7.4
Georgia	7.3
Massachusetts	7.3
New Hampshire	7.3
Tennessee	7.3
Arizona	7.2
Connecticut	7.2
South Dakota	7.2
Texas	7.2
Wyoming	7.2
Illinois	7.1
Alabama	7.0
Louisiana	7.0
Missouri	7.0
North Carolina	7.0
South Carolina	7.0
California	6.9
Michigan	6.9
Minnesota	6.9
Nebraska	6.9
New Jersey	6.9
Pennsylvania	6.9
Alberta	6.8
Kansas	6.8
Wisconsin	6.8
Florida	6.7
Ohio	6.7
Oregon	6.7
Utah	6.7
Kentucky	6.6
New York	6.6
Idaho	6.5
Vermont	6.5
Virginia	6.5
Washington	6.5
Hawaii	6.4
Iowa	6.4
Maryland	6.3
Mississippi	6.3
Oklahoma	6.3
Rhode Island	6.2
Alaska	6.1
Arkansas	6.1
New Mexico	6.0
North Dakota	5.8
Maine	5.7
Montana	5.6
West Virginia	5.6
Ontario	5.5
British Columbia	4.7
Nova Scotia	4.6
Newfoundland	4.5
New Brunswick	4.4
Saskatchewan	4.4
Manitoba	4.1
Quebec	4.1
Prince Edward Island	3.4

Level of Economic Freedom

Figure 2: Summary of 2000 Ratings—Subnational

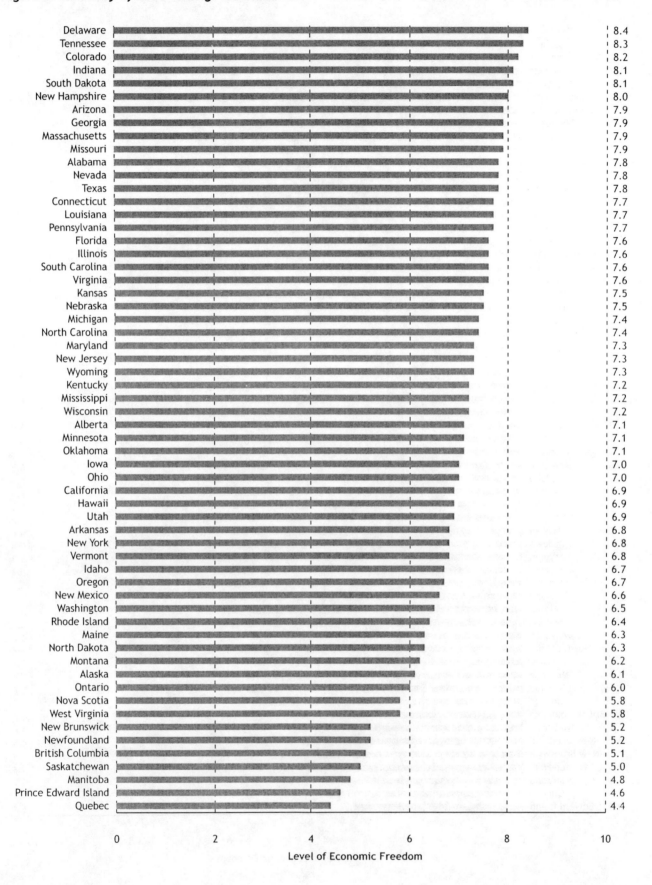

	Level of Economic Freedom
Delaware	8.4
Tennessee	8.3
Colorado	8.2
Indiana	8.1
South Dakota	8.1
New Hampshire	8.0
Arizona	7.9
Georgia	7.9
Massachusetts	7.9
Missouri	7.9
Alabama	7.8
Nevada	7.8
Texas	7.8
Connecticut	7.7
Louisiana	7.7
Pennsylvania	7.7
Florida	7.6
Illinois	7.6
South Carolina	7.6
Virginia	7.6
Kansas	7.5
Nebraska	7.5
Michigan	7.4
North Carolina	7.4
Maryland	7.3
New Jersey	7.3
Wyoming	7.3
Kentucky	7.2
Mississippi	7.2
Wisconsin	7.2
Alberta	7.1
Minnesota	7.1
Oklahoma	7.1
Iowa	7.0
Ohio	7.0
California	6.9
Hawaii	6.9
Utah	6.9
Arkansas	6.8
New York	6.8
Vermont	6.8
Idaho	6.7
Oregon	6.7
New Mexico	6.6
Washington	6.5
Rhode Island	6.4
Maine	6.3
North Dakota	6.3
Montana	6.2
Alaska	6.1
Ontario	6.0
Nova Scotia	5.8
West Virginia	5.8
New Brunswick	5.2
Newfoundland	5.2
British Columbia	5.1
Saskatchewan	5.0
Manitoba	4.8
Prince Edward Island	4.6
Quebec	4.4

domestic product (GDP) in each jurisdiction and thus do not require translation between exchange rates. The exception is the income-tax rate variable, where the exchange rate is used to calculate equivalent top thresholds in Canada and the United States.

Description of Variables

Using a simple mathematical formula to reduce subjective judgments, a scale from zero to 10 was constructed to represent the underlying distribution of the nine variables in the index. Ten is the highest possible score and indicates a high level of economic freedom.[5] Thus, this *index* is a relative ranking. The rating formula is consistent across time to allow an examination of the evolution of economic freedom. To construct the overall index without imposing subjective judgments about the relative importance of the variable, each area was equally weighted and each variable within each area was equally weighted (see Appendix C: Methodology (p. 51) for more details).

The index developed in this paper assigns a higher score of economic freedom when a government size variable is smaller in one state or province relative to another. This would seem to contradict the theory of economic freedom, which does not predict that a government size of zero maximizes freedom. Indeed, important government functions, such as the enforcement of the rule of law, are necessary for economic freedom and freedom more broadly. However, all the theory of economic freedom requires is that governments be large enough to undertake an adequate but minimal level of the "protective" and "productive" functions of government, discussed in the next section. It is unlikely that any government considered in this sample is too small to perform these functions at the minimum required level.

In examining the areas below, it may seem that Areas 1 and 2 create a double counting, in that they capture the two sides of the government ledger sheet, revenues and expenditures, which presumably should balance over time. However, in examining subnational jurisdictions, this situation does not hold. In the United States, and even more so in Canada, a number of intergovernmental transfers break the link between taxation and spending at the subnational level.[6] The break between revenues and spending is even more pronounced at the all-government level, which includes the federal government. Obviously, what the federal government spends in a state or a province does not necessarily bear a strong relationship to the amount of money it raises in that jurisdiction. Thus, to take examples from both Canada and the United States, the respective federal governments spend more in Newfoundland and West Virginia than they raise through taxation in these jurisdictions. The opposite pattern occurs for Alberta and Connecticut.

As discussed below, both taxation and spending can suppress economic freedom. Since the link between the two is broken when examining subnational jurisdictions, it is necessary to examine both sides of the government's balance sheet.

Area 1: Size of Government
1A: General Consumption Expenditures by Government as a Percentage of GDP

As the size of government expands, less room is available for private choice. While government can fulfill useful roles in society, there is a tendency for government to undertake superfluous activities as it expands. According to Gwartney et al. "there are two broad functions of government that are consistent with economic freedom: (1) protection of individuals against invasions by intruders, both domestic and foreign, and (2) provision of a few selected goods—what economists call public goods" (1996: 22).

These two broad functions of government are often called protective and productive functions of government. Once government moves beyond these two functions into provision of private goods, goods that can be produced by private firms and individuals, they restrict consumer choice and, thus, economic freedom (Gwartney et al. 1996). In other words, government spending, independent of taxation, by itself reduces economic freedom once this spending exceeds what is necessary to provide a minimal level of protective and productive functions. Thus, as the size of government consumption grows a jurisdiction receives a lower score in this component.

1B: Transfers and Subsidies as a Percentage of GDP

When the government taxes one person in order to give money to another, it separates individuals from the full benefits of their labor and reduces the real returns of such activity (Gwartney et al. 1996). These transfers represent the removal of property without providing a compensating benefit and are, thus, an infringement on economic freedom. Put another way, when governments take from one group in order to give to another, they are violating the same property rights they are supposed to protect. The greater the level of transfers and subsidies, the lower the score a jurisdiction receives.

Area 2: Takings and Discriminatory Taxation
2A: Total Government Revenue from Own Source as a Percentage of GDP;

2B: Top Marginal Income Tax Rate[7] and the Income Threshold at Which It Applies;

2C: Indirect Taxes as a Percentage of GDP;

2D: Sales Taxes Collected as a Percentage of GDP.

Some form of government funding is necessary to support the functions of government but, as the tax burden grows, the restrictions on private choice increase and thus economic freedom declines. Taxes that have a discriminatory impact and bear little reference to services received infringe on economic freedom even more. "High marginal tax rates discriminate against productive citizens and deny them the fruits of their labor" (Gwartney et al. 1996: 30). In each of the above variables, a higher rate lowers a jurisdiction's score in this component. Top personal income tax rates are also rated by the income thresholds at which they apply. Higher thresholds result in a better score.

Examining the separate sources of government revenue gives the reader more information than just examining a single tax source or overall taxes. Nonetheless, total own-source revenue is included to pick up the impact of taxes, particularly various corporate and capital taxes, not included in the other three variables.

Area 3: Labor Market Freedom
3A: Minimum Wage Legislation

High minimum wages restrict the ability of employers and employees to negotiate contracts to their liking. In particular, minimum wage legislation restricts the ability of low-skilled workers and workforce entrants to negotiate for employment they might otherwise accept, and thus minimum wage laws most restrict the economic freedom of workers in these groups and the employers who might otherwise hire them.

This component measures the annual income earned by someone working at the minimum wage as a ratio of per-capita GDP. Since per-capita GDP is a proxy for the average productivity in a jurisdiction, this ratio takes into account differences in the ability to pay wages across jurisdictions. As the minimum wage grows relative to productivity, thus narrowing the range of employment contracts that can be freely negotiated, there are further reductions in economic freedom, resulting in a lower score for the jurisdiction. For example, minimum wage legislation set at 0.1% of average productivity is likely to have no impact on economic freedom; set at 50% of average productivity, the legislation would limit the freedom of workers and firms to negotiate employment to a much greater extent. Put another way, a minimum wage requirement of $2 an hour for New York will have little impact but, for a third world nation, it might remove most potential workers from the effective workforce. The same idea holds, though in a narrower range, for jurisdictions within North America.

3B: Government Employment as a Percentage of Total State/Provincial Employment

Economic freedom decreases for several reasons as government employment increases beyond what is necessary for government's productive and protective functions. Government, in effect, is using expropriated money to take an amount of labor out of the labor market. This restricts the ability of individuals and organizations to contract freely for labor services since potential employers have to bid against their own tax dollars in attempting to obtain labor. High levels of government employment may also indicate that government is attempting to supply goods and services that individuals contracting freely with each other could provide on their own. It may also be that the government is attempting to provide goods and services that individuals would not care to obtain if able to contract freely. It may also indicate that government is engaging in regulatory and other activities that restrict the freedom of citizens. Finally, high levels of government employment suggest government is directly undertaking work that could be contracted privately. When government, instead of funding private providers, decides to provide directly a good or service, it reduces economic freedom by limiting choice and by typically creating a government quasi-monopoly in provision of services. For instance, the creation of school vouchers may not decrease government expenditures but it will reduce government employment, eroding government's monopoly on the provision of publicly funded education services while creating more choice for parents and students and, thus, enhancing economic freedom.

3C: Occupational Licensing

As the number of regulated occupations expand, the mobility of labor is reduced. Often those certified in one jurisdiction have difficulty getting certified in another. If there are barriers to movement of qualified labor from one place to another within a country, then economic freedom is reduced. Moreover, in many cases restrictions on entry into a profession serve little public benefit; instead, they may be enacted for the benefit of the regulated group, which is able to maintain a monopoly on certain types of work so that other individuals may not freely contract with whom they might choose. These laws often protect the interests of "insiders" from potential competition. A greater number of regulated occupations results in a lower score for a jurisdiction.

Each of the variables above exists in the two dimensions we have already mentioned: the subnational and the all-government level. Total revenue from own sources, for example, is calculated first for local/municipal and provincial/state governments, and then again counting all levels of government that capture revenue from individuals living in a given province or state.

Notes

1 See Easton and Walker 1997, De Haan and Sturm 2000, and other related papers at www. freetheworld.com.

2 A listing of many of these books and additional information can be found at www. freetheworld.com.

3 Knox 2002.

4 See Gwartney et al. 2002. The website www. freetheworld.com has references to a number of important papers and books that explore the theory of economic freedom.

5 Due to the way variables are calculated, a mini-max procedure discussed in Appendix C: Methodology (p. 51), 10 is not indicative of perfect economic freedom.

6 Most governments have revenue sources other than taxation and national governments also have international financial obligations so that the relation between taxation and spending will not be exactly one-to-one, even at the national level. Nevertheless, over time, the relationship will be close for most national governments, except those receiving large amounts of foreign aid.

7 See Appendix C: Methodology (p. 51) for further discussion of how the variable for the top marginal tax rate and its threshold was derived.

Chapter 2: Overview of the Results

Prior to a detailed discussion of the econometric testing, we will present some simple graphics for illustrative purposes. These charts dramatically demonstrate the important links between prosperity and economic freedom, links that are more fully explored in the econometric testing.

Figure 3 breaks economic freedom into quintiles at the all-government level. For example, the category on the far left of the chart, "Bottom," represents the jurisdictions that score in the lowest fifth of the economic freedom ratings, the 12 lowest of the 60 North American jurisdictions. Nine of these are Canadian provinces—all except Alberta. The jurisdictions in this bottom quintile have an average per-capita GDP of just US$21,056 (C$31,265). This compares to an average per-capita GDP of US$37,268 (C$55,337) for the 12 top-ranked jurisdictions.

Figure 4 is the same chart type as Figure 3 but represents economic freedom at the subnational level. Here, the bottom quintile has an average per-capita GDP of $22,383 (C$33,236) compared to the top quintile with an average per-capita GDP of $35,321 (C$52,446). As will be noted in the econometric testing, economic freedom has a smaller impact at the subnational level than at the all-government level. This is expected since only at the all-government level are all government restrictions on economic freedom captured.

Another useful way to review economic freedom is through deviation from the mean. This examines the impact on economic activity of a jurisdiction's being above or below the average ranking of other national jurisdictions, comparing Canadian provinces with the Canadian average and US states with the US average. Here scatter charts help illustrate the point, though a quick visual inspection will show these diagrams could easily be translated into column graphs like Figures 3 and 4.

Figure 3: Economic Freedom at an All-Government Level and per-Capita GDP

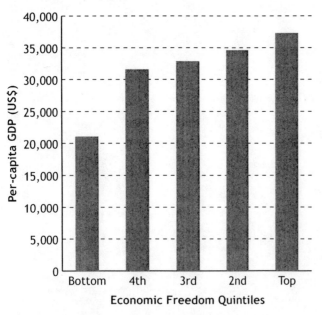

Figure 4: Economic Freedom at a Subnational Level and per-Capita GDP

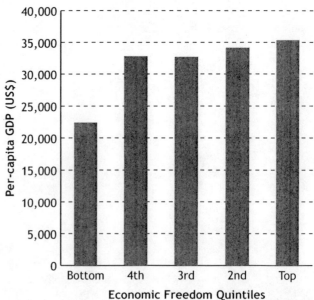

Figures 5 and 6 relate prosperity to economic freedom, with economic freedom plotted along the horizontal axis and per-capita GDP plotted along the vertical axis. Once again these charts illustrate the connection between economic freedom and prosperity. Here too, as expected, the subnational relationship is weaker than the all-government one.

Finally, in this illustrative section, we look at the relationship between growth of economic freedom and the growth of a jurisdiction's economy, another topic more fully explored in the following testing. In Figures 7 and 8, changes in economic freedom are plotted along the horizontal axis while changes in economic growth are plotted along the vertical axis. Again, the expected relationships are found, with economic growth strongly linked to growth in economic freedom.

Comparing the Two Indexes

In general, rankings at an all-government level are not drastically different from rankings at a subnational level when US states, as a group, are compared with Canadian provinces, as a group. This is partly due to the way the subnational variable is constructed. Subnational responsibilities in Canada and the United States differ. Thus, government spending and taxation patterns cannot be directly compared. Instead, an "adjustment factor," explained in Appendix D: Adjustment Factors (p. 53), is used. One effect of this adjustment factor is to give Canadian provinces, on average, similar relative rankings to US states in both indexes. Nonetheless, the two indexes produce different results when the rankings of individual states and provinces is examined.

Rankings at a subnational level for individual Canadian provinces change somewhat when moving from the all-government to subnational levels. For example, in 2000, Nova Scotia, and New Brunswick decreased their ratings from 52nd and 54th at a subnational level to 54th and 56th, respectively, at an all-government level. Alberta and British Columbia, on the other hand, increased their ratings from 31st and 56th at a subnational level to 26th and 53rd, respectively, at an all-government level. In the United States in 2000, Virginia, Maryland, and Mississippi decrease their ratings from 17th, 25th, and 28th at a subnational level to 35th, 41st, and 41st, respectively, at an all-government level. Wyoming, California, and Oregon improved their ratings from 25th, 36th, and 42nd at a subnational level to 9th, 20th, and 29th, respectively, at an all-government level in 2000. Other states and provinces changed their ratings from subnational to all-government level and vice versa less drastically.

The Evolution of Economic Freedom in North America

As can be seen from Tables 1 and 2, the evolution of economic freedom in North America follows an expected pattern. In the United States, at the all-government level, economic freedom increases through the 1980s, coinciding with the Reagan era. It then falls in the early 1990s, following tax increases under the Bush and early Clinton administrations and then begins to rise again. At the subnational level, the pattern is the same but less pronounced, again as one might expect. Many states embarked upon Reagan-like government restructuring, but not all, and often not at the same level of intensity, or in the same time frame.[1]

Table 1 *Average Economic Freedom Scores at an All-Government Level*

	1981	1985	1989	1993	1994	1995	1996	1997	1998	1999	2000
Canada	4.0	4.1	4.4	3.8	3.9	4.1	4.2	4.3	4.4	4.5	4.7
US	6.3	6.5	7.0	6.7	6.6	6.6	6.7	6.7	6.7	6.7	6.8
Difference	2.3	2.4	2.6	2.9	2.7	2.5	2.5	2.4	2.3	2.2	2.1

Table 2 *Average Economic Freedom Scores at a Subnational Level*

	1981	1985	1989	1993	1994	1995	1996	1997	1998	1999	2000
Canada	4.8	4.7	4.8	4.1	4.4	4.5	4.7	4.9	5.1	5.3	5.3
US	7.1	7.1	7.2	6.8	7.0	6.9	7.0	7.1	7.2	7.3	7.3
Difference	2.3	2.4	2.4	2.7	2.6	2.4	2.3	2.2	2.1	2.0	2.0

Figure 5: Average per-Capita GDP and Average Economic Freedom at an All-Government Level

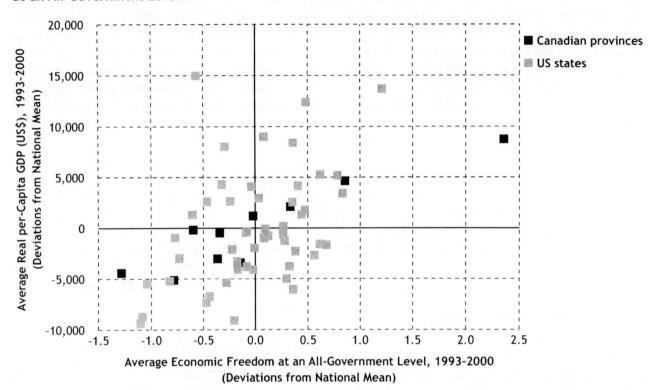

Figure 6: Average per-Capita GDP and Average Economic Freedom at a Subnational Level

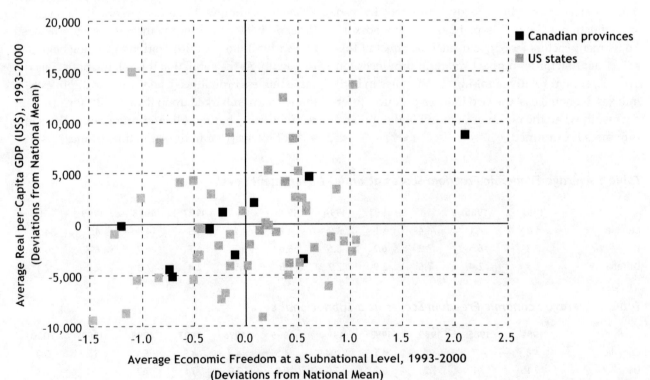

Figure 7: Average Growth in per-Capita GDP and Average Growth in Economic Freedom at an All-Government Level

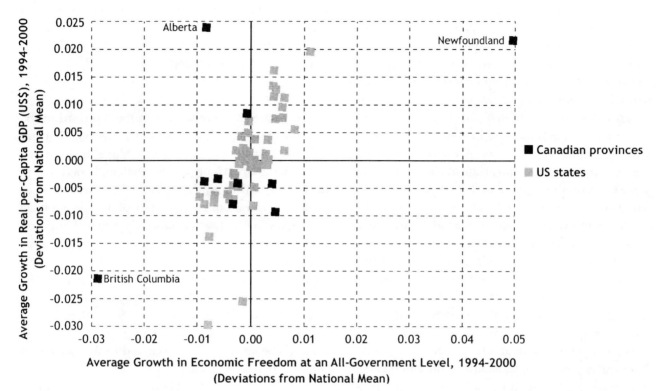

Figure 8: Average Growth in per-Capita GDP and Average Growth in Economic Freedom at a Subnational Level

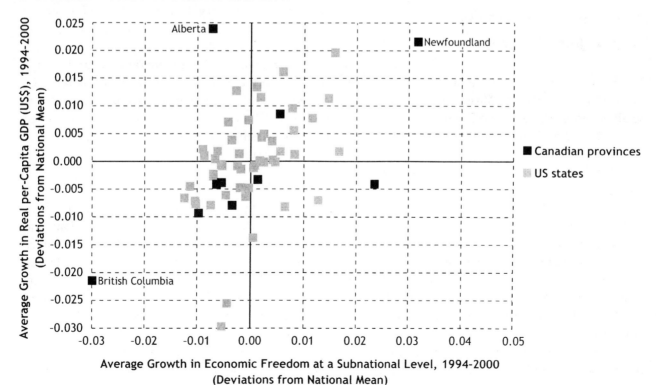

In Canada through the 1980s, economic freedom remained fairly constant at the subnational level while it increased somewhat at the all-government level, perhaps as a result of a change of federal government, and a resulting change in policy, in 1984. In both indexes, economic freedom falls in Canada in the early 1990s and then begins to rise. In early 1990s, federal, provincial, and municipal governments began to address their debts and deficits but typically more through increased taxation than through lower spending. However, as debts and deficits were brought under control, governments began to reduce some tax rates through the mid-, and particularly the late, 1990s. Also in this period, fiscally conservative governments were elected in Canada's two richest provinces, Alberta and Ontario.

Overall patterns in Canada and the United States are similar. Both nations fought debts and deficits in the early 1990s with tax increases. However, Canada raised taxes more aggressively as can be seen in the increasing gaps in economic freedom in the two nations during this period. From 1981 to 2000, the gap between Canada and the United States in economic freedom at the subnational and the all-government level first rose and then fell back to just below its 1981 level.

Overview of the Results for the United States

US states can move up and down in the rankings quite substantially. For instance, Massachusetts was 47th in the all-government index and 34th in the subnational index in 1981, the beginning of the period under study. By 2000, it risen to the 5th in the all-government index and 7th in the subnational index. Massachusetts state income rose with the increase in economic freedom, from an income below the national average to one tied for 2nd highest in 2000.

Oklahoma's economic freedom suffered the worst decline. In 1981, it was 5th in the all-government index and 10th in the subnational index. By 2000, it has declined to 41st and 31st, and state income had fell from the 10th highest in the nation to the bottom of the ranks at 46th.

Although the econometric work in this paper shows a strong and highly significant link between economic freedom and economic activity, a link found in the vast majority of states, exceptions to this relationship also occur, since any number of external factors such as resource wealth and proximity to transportation routes affect economic growth. Such outriders will be discussed below.

Top States

Several states have remained in the top third of the rankings through all or most of the period. They are Delaware (since the late 1980s), Colorado, Tennessee, Nevada, Indiana, Georgia, Connecticut, Texas (though its relative rank among the top 16 states has deteriorated sharply), and Louisiana. A few of these states have per-capita GDP below the national average though, on average, the states in the top third exceed the US average per-capita GDP by 8%. Moreover, all consistently high-ranked states have seen their per-capita GDP increase relative to the national average, except Nevada, Louisiana and Texas, though for Texas this decline accompanied a relative weakening in economic freedom. (Whenever GDP is discussed in this section, it refers to per-capita GDP.)

Two states, New Hampshire, which gained sharply in the rankings over the period, and Georgia, which has been consistently free, have risen from just over 80% of the national per-capita GDP in 1981 to 109% and 115%, respectively. Massachusetts is an even more interesting story. In 1981, its level of economic freedom was among the worst of the states and its per-capita GDP was well below the national average. It improved its economic freedom rankings and income went up. In the early 1990s, Massachusetts reversed course again and both economic freedom and relative income fell. More recently, Massachusetts has moved up rapidly in the rankings to become one of the freest and richest states.

The Middle Ranks

The middling states, roughly speaking, have remained middling in both economic freedom and economic activity through most of the period. Since the late 1980s, most of these 17 states have had more or less stable economic freedom rankings while the average per-capita GDP of these states has not varied from the national average by much more than a percentage point.

There are exceptions. New Jersey and Michigan moved up in the rankings sharply, typically by 15 spots or more on both indexes. Both have also improved their per-capita GDP relative to the national average substantially. Florida is the only middling state, which fell by more than 10 rankings in both indexes, although its GDP has risen slightly against the national average.

Iowa, Mississippi, and Oklahoma are in the middle third of the subnational rankings and the bottom third of the all-government rankings. All three have declined in the rankings substantially. Oklahoma, as noted above, suffered the largest decline among the states. It has also suffered the greatest fall in per-capita GDP, from 7% above the national average to 12% below it. Iowa has also declined in both rankings and relative GDP substantially. Mississippi's economic freedom ranking rose into the early 1990s and then fell sharply. Its per-capita GDP relative to the rest of the nation followed the same pattern.

The Worst Performers

Some states seem to want to keep economic freedom at bay. West Virginia has by far the worst record. It also has the lowest per-capita GDP in the United States and has the worst economic record of all states through the 1990s. For Montana and North Dakota, the rejection of economic freedom is a relatively new taste. Both have gone from the middle of the pack to battling West Virginia for bottom spot. Over the same period, Montana and North Dakota have seen their per-capita GDP decline by 23 and 31 percentage points, respectively, against the national average. Other consistent under performers include Maine, New Mexico, Arkansas, Alaska, and Rhode Island.

The Outriders

Economic freedom does not, nor is it meant to, capture all things that affect economic activity. Thus other factors, resource wealth for instance, will break the strong relationship between economic freedom and economic activity discussed here and shown in the econometric testing. Among the outriders are Louisiana, with a weaker economy than its level of economic freedom would suggest, and Alaska and New York, with the opposite pattern. Indiana has weak economic growth compared to its high level of economic freedom. The purpose here is not to explain these anomalies—that would require a detailed discussion of each of state's economy—but rather to draw the reader's attention to the fact that exceptions exist.

Overview of the Canadian Results

Canadian provinces consistently have lower scores than US states and thus are clustered near the bottom of the ranking.

Top Provinces

Alberta is the only province that has consistently done better than at least some states. It ranked 26th at an all-government level and 31st at a subnational level in 2000. Although Alberta's economic freedom declined through the 1980s and early 1990s, in all years it has remained ahead of at least one state, usually West Virginia, in the rankings of both indexes. Alberta's lowest scores and rankings were 1989 and 1993. Since then, Alberta's score and ranking in both indexes have improved considerably.

Ontario placed ahead of three states at the all-government level in 1981 and one state, West Virginia, in 1985. At the subnational level, it ranked ahead of several states in the 1980s. However, in the late 1980s and early 1990s, Ontario's economic freedom declined sharply. Economic freedom recovered through the mid- and late 1990s but only the 2000 scores show Ontario regaining, roughly speaking, the level of economic freedom it had in 1981. Over the same period, average scores in the United States also rose, leaving Ontario further behind the US average than it was two decades ago. Ontario is now behind all states in the all-government index and ahead of only one state, West Virginia, in the subnational rankings.

The Middle Ranks

Despite declines in economic freedom relative to the rest of the nation, this deterioration was not large enough to push British Columbia below the 3rd highest ranking among Canadian provinces at the all-government level throughout the full period discussed in this report. However, at the subnational level, both British Columbia's score and ranking deteriorated relative to other Canadian provinces, falling to 6th spot among the provinces in 2000.

Manitoba's ranking has consistently trended downwards in both indexes, from roughly the middle of the Canadian pack in 1981 to the bottom rungs in 2000. The opposite pattern is found for New Brunswick, Newfoundland, and Nova Scotia, which roughly speaking have moved up from the bottom rungs to the middle of the pack.

The Worst Performers

On average, Prince Edward Island has been the second worst performer in Canada. Since 1994, it has scored dead last in the all-government index. In the subnational index, it has been the second last since 1998. Overall, Quebec has been the worst performing province. In the subnational rankings, Quebec has been in last spot for all years. At the all-government level, Quebec has been close to the bottom of the pack since 1993.

Canadian Fiscal Federalism

The Government of Canada may well be unique in the amount of money it transfers among provinces and regions. For example, in Canada's Atlantic Provinces, the nation's most economically depressed region, *net* federal spending—the difference between federal revenues raised in the region and the amount of federal spending—typically equaled between 20% and 40% of regional GDP during the period under consideration. Although transfers between levels of government occur within the United States, the magnitude of these transfers is much smaller than in Canada.[2]

Inter-regional transfers in Canada create a fiscal drain on "have" regions. This is obvious at the federal level where tax revenues are in effect transferred from "have" to "have-not" provinces but it also occurs at the provincial level. The federal taxation burden reduces room for provincial taxation in all provinces. This is a significant problem for "have" provinces but not for "have-not" provinces since a considerable portion of federal transfers to "have-not" regions go directly to provincial governments, which are thus more than compensated for the loss of taxation room.

Nonetheless, one would expect that most of the negative impact of fiscal federalism would be found at the all-government level, which directly includes the impact of federal taxation and transfers. Indeed, this is what the data show. This is unfortunate because it is at the all-government level, which calculates the impact of all governments on economic freedom, where the effects of economic freedom are strongest.

The results of fiscal federalism on economic freedom in Canada can be seen most clearly when examining Alberta and Ontario, the economically freest of the Canadian provinces. The point can be illustrated by examining the most recent data for the year 2000, at the all-government level, which includes the impact of the federal government and thus the impact of fiscal federalism on these provinces. Recall that high scores indicate low levels of taxation and expenditure, and vice versa.

In Area 1: Size of Government, Alberta and Ontario score quite highly in both the all-government and the subnational levels, at least for Canadian provinces. These comparatively good scores indicate relatively low levels of government expenditures in both provinces. If these levels of government spending indicate the preference of voters in these provinces for economic freedom, then both provinces would score highly in the overall index, if provincial voters were able to assert control over the province's fiscal decisions. Yet, fiscal federalism erodes the sovereignty of the electorate.

Despite the low levels of government spending, high levels of taxation dramatically reduce Ontario and Alberta's overall scores, possibly frustrating their electorates taste for economic freedom. At the all-government level, Alberta has the 10th best score on government spending while Ontario has the 24th best score in 2000. But taxation levels are much higher than the amount of government expenditure would indicate. In the Area 2: Takings and Discriminatory Taxation, Alberta falls to 15th spot while Ontario falls to 52nd spot. A comparison between these scores highlights both the low level of federal spending in these provinces and the high level of federal taxation.

High levels of taxation can occur even in cases of low government spending in Canada because the federal government transfers dollars from rich provinces to poor provinces. Given the relationship between economic freedom prosperity, this in effect means the federal government is transferring money from provinces with high levels of economic freedom to provinces with low levels of economic freedom. This perverse reward pattern frustrates the growth ability of economically free provinces and rewards provinces for limiting economic freedom.

Explaining a Puzzle

Canadian fiscal federalism may help explain a puzzle found in the following discussion of the econometric results. The impact of economic freedom on Canadian provinces is considerably weaker than on US states at both the all-government and subnational level. This may be because of the interaction between Canada's fiscal structure, economic freedom, and economic growth.

To understand the impact of Canada's fiscal federalism, consider a province that reduces economic freedom by, for example, increasing taxes. This will likely have a negative impact on the provincial economy, as both the following results and international testing show. However, the weaker provincial economy means the province will receive an increase in federal payouts (or a reduction in the fiscal outflow if the province in question is a "have" province). The greater the reduction in economic freedom, the greater the negative impact on the economy and the greater the amount of money the province will receive from the federal government. This inflow of funds will, at least in the short term, partly offset the negative impact on GDP and mute the impact of economic freedom, or its loss, on the economy. (In the longer term, the inflow of funds will also weaken the economy but this impact is likely beyond the time horizon of the tests conducted here.)

On the other hand, if a province increases economic freedom, for example by reducing taxes, and its economy grows, the result is an increased outflow of government revenues to other jurisdictions and a heavier tax burden, given the progressively of Canadian taxes, which in turn suppresses increases in economic freedom and economic growth. In other words, fiscal federalism mutes the impact of economic freedom in Canada. Economic growth itself, because of Canada's fiscal structure, reduces a province's economic freedom and thus brakes further growth. Despite the problems created by Canada's fiscal structure, economic freedom still proves to be a powerful stimulant for increasing prosperity in Canada.

Impact of Fiscal Federalism

Unfortunately, Canada's fiscal federalism seems to harm both rich and poor provinces. The discussion above shows how fiscal federalism frustrates the ability of some provinces to improve their economic freedom and, thus, their prosperity. However, the effects are at least as unfortunate in the poorer provinces, where a rich menu of government spending pushes out other economic activity and politicizes the economy. As a result, the rate of convergence[3] of Canada's poorer regions is about a third to a half of the rate of convergence of poor regions in the United States, Europe, and Japan. (See Barro and Sala-I-Martin 1995 for international results on convergence.)

The incentives created by fiscal federalism are also damaging. Because fiscal federalism mutes the ability of provinces to move towards economic freedom and thus weakens the positive impact of economic freedom, the incentive for provinces to increase the freedom of their economies weakens.

Even worse, the elites in "have-not" provinces have incentives to limit economic freedom. Low levels of economic freedom reduce economic activity and increase the flow of federal transfers. These transfers are predominately captured by the political and business elites, meaning they face incentives to keep economic growth low. As well, Canada's Employment Insurance system alters the incentives facing many voters, since they can benefit from the structure of the EI system, which also weakens economic growth by removing large segments of the population from the year-round workforce so long as economic activity remains weak.

While all segments of the population would deny being influenced by such incentives, there has been no significant economic reform movement in Atlantic Canada, even though there is much evidence from around the world that the region's policy mix damages growth.

Notes

1 Gwartney and Lawson (2002) show steadily rising scores for Canada and the United States through this period. This is because of variables that can only be examined at the national level, such as price level. Obviously, states and provinces do not have their own independent monetary policy.

2 A discussion of fiscal federalism can be found in McMahon 2000b: chapter 3. The US fiscal structure is discussed in McMahon 2000a: chapter 4.

3 The rate of convergence is the rate at which poorer jurisdictions catch up to richer ones.

Chapter 3: The Relationship between Economic Freedom and Economic Well-Being

A number of studies have linked levels of economic freedom with higher levels of economic growth and income. Easton and Walker (1997) found that changes in economic freedom have a significant impact on the steady-state level of income even after the level of technology, the level of education of the workforce, and the level of investment are taken into account. The results of this study imply that economic freedom is a separate determinant of the level of income. The Fraser Institute's series, *Economic Freedom of the World*, also shows a positive relationship between economic freedom and both the level of per-capita GDP and its growth rate.

De Haan and Sturm (2000) show that positive and negative changes in economic freedom lead to positive and negative changes in economic growth rates. Using the economic freedom index from Gwartney et al. (1996) and per-capita GDP data for 80 countries, their results indicate that after accounting for education level, investment, and population growth, changes in economic freedom have a significant impact on economic growth. The calculation of the index of the economic freedom of North America allows us for the first time to investigate the relationship between economic freedom and prosperity within North America.

To test whether or not there is a positive relationship between economic growth and economic freedom, we use annual observations on each of the variables from 1993 to 2000. We run separate regressions for Canada and the United States to determine if economic freedom has different effects in the two nations. As the data for all US states and all Canadian provinces were used, the study is one of a defined population rather than a random sample of states and provinces, implying that the appropriate estimation technique is the fixed effects, rather than the random effects, model.

Tables 3 and 4 show the regression results of the semi-growth models. Please note that the coefficients on regressions testing the level of GDP and economic freedom represent US dollars. In the regressions for Canadian provinces, these coefficients are translated into Canadian dollars, using the exchange rate in the year 2000.

Average investment share of GDP is missing from the model because investment data for separate US states is not available.[1] The proxy variable for human capital in our model is not statistically significant. Since the investment variable is missing from the model and the proxy variable for human capital is not significant, the data have to be adjusted. The fixed effects model captures the unobserved or ignorance effects. It does not, however, account for missing relevant variables from a model.

To provide some adjustment for missing relevant variables, the data are transformed into deviations from their national means. In other words, the national mean is subtracted from each of the variables. Although this transformation does not adjust for the omission of the relevant variables completely, to the extent that jurisdictions within a national context are similarly affected by the same economic factors, the transformation—which reveals how each jurisdiction performs in relation to the national average—helps adjust for the impact of the missing relevant variables on other explanatory variables in the model.

The results from the regression analysis in Table 3 indicate that the economic freedom level has a substantial impact on per-capita GDP at a subnational and all-government level. The high school variable is not significant. The reader should also note the relatively small standard errors for the economic freedom variable, both in the regression results reported here and for those reported in the Sensitivity Analysis section, later in this paper. On the whole, the US results are more statistically significant than the Canadian results, though even the Canadian results typically have a *p*-value below 1%, meaning the results, roughly speaking, are statistically significant more than 99 times out

Table 3: Economic Freedom Level and Per-Capita GDP[2]

Regressions at All-Government Level (ALLG)					**Regressions at Subnational Level (SUBN)**				
Dependent Variable: Per Capita GDP (1993-2000)					Dependent Variable: Per Capita GDP (1993-2000)				
Method: Pooled Least Squares					Method: Pooled Least Squares				
Sample: 1993-2000					Sample: 1993-2000				
Canada									
Total panel (balanced) observations: 80					Total panel (balanced) observations: 80				
Variable	Coefficient	Std. Error	t-Statistic	Prob.	Variable	Coefficient	Std. Error	t-Statistic	Prob.
HG	3.91	8.69	0.45	0.65	HG	–6.16	8.61	–0.72	0.48
ALLG	2558.11 (C$3,798.42)	461.20	5.55	0.00	SUBN	1859.36 (C$2,760.88)	414.01	4.49	0.00
Adjusted R^2: 0.98					Adjusted R^2: 0.98				
United States									
Total panel (balanced) observations: 400					Total panel (balanced) observations: 400				
Variable	Coefficient	Std. Error	t-Statistic	Prob.	Variable	Coefficient	Std. Error	t-Statistic	Prob.
HG	–3.46	2.99	–1.16	0.25	HG	–1.10	3.73	–0.29	0.77
ALLG	7185.32	377.59	19.03	0.00	SUBN	3327. 68	321.66	10.35	0.00
Adjusted R^2: 0.98					Adjusted R^2: 0.97				

Notes

HG is the number of high school graduates per 10,000 people (25 years and older) from 1993 to 2000;

ALLG is an economic freedom index at an all-government level from 1993 to 2000;

SUBN is an economic freedom index at a subnational level from 1993 to 2000.

of 100. Somewhat lower statistical significance on the Canadian tests may reflect both the nature of Canada's fiscal federalism, which mutes the effects of economic freedom, and the fact there are obviously more data points for 50 states than 10 provinces.

At an all-government level, holding other variables constant, an increase of one point in economic freedom in a US state will increase that state's per-capita income by US $7,185. An increase of one point in economic freedom in a Canadian province will increase its per-capita GDP by US$2,558 (C$3,798.42). At a subnational level, an increase of one point in economic freedom in a US state will increase its per-capita GDP by US$3,328, whereas an increase of one point in economic freedom in a Canadian province will increase its per-capita GDP by US$1,859 (C$2,760.88).

For both Canada and the United States, the impact of economic freedom on per-capita GDP is higher at an all-government level than it is at a subnational level. This is the expected result, since the all-government variable captures the impact of restrictions on economic freedom imposed at both the subnational and all-government levels.

While the coefficients may appear quite large, it should be noted that the overall index varies much less than its individual components, so that a one-point overall increase in economic freedom may not be as easy to achieve as might appear at first notice. The difference in scores between the highest and lowest rated state over the full period is only 2.49 points at the all-government level. Thus a US state would have to improve its score by roughly 40% within this range in order to achieve the one point increase required to realize the $7,185 per-capita gain in income. In Canada, at the all-government level, the range is 4.07. At the subnational level, the range in Canada is 3.78; in the United States, it is 3.02.

The broader range of variation in Canada may help explain part, though not all, of the differences in the size of the coefficients on economic freedom between the two nations. The coefficient is the number that describes the economic impact of economic freedom. The coefficient on economic freedom at the all-government level is 181% larger for the US states than for Canadian provinces (7185 versus 2558). However, the Canadian range of variation is only 63% greater than the US range of variation (2.49 versus 4.07). Similarly, at the subnational level, the US coefficient is 79% greater than coefficient for Canadian provinces while the range of variation in Canada is only 25% greater than the US range of variation. Thus, the difference in the range of variation cannot completely explain the difference in the magnitude of the coefficients. As discussed earlier, the structure of Canada's fiscal federalism is the likely explanation for the weaker impact of economic freedom in Canada, particularly at the all-government level.

Table 4 summarizes the results of the regression analysis used to determine the relationship between growth in economic freedom and growth in per-capita GDP at a subnational and all-government level. The main conclusion of the regression analysis results is that growth in economic freedom has a significant impact on the growth in per-capita GDP.

At an all-government level, a one-percent increase in the growth of economic freedom in US states will increase the growth rate of per-capita GDP by 1% whereas a one-percent increase in the growth of economic freedom in a Canadian province will increase growth rate of per-capita GDP by 0.52%. At a subnational level, a one-percent increase in growth in economic freedom in US states will increase growth rate of per-capita GDP by 0.48% whereas a 1% increase

in the growth of the economic freedom in a Canadian province will increase growth rate in per-capita GDP by 0.40%. At a subnational level, growth in economic freedom has the almost the same impact on US states and the Canadian provinces. As noted, the impact of Canada's fiscal federal will be smaller at the subnational than all-government levels. This could be due to the adjustment of the Canadian data at a sub national level (see Appendix D, Adjustment Factors, p. 53). Note that for the US states and the Canadian provinces growth in economic freedom has a larger impact at an all-government level than at a subnational level.

Here again, it is important to consider the range of growth of economic freedom over the period. For Canada, at the all-government level, the range is 22% compared to 10% in the United States. For Canada, at the subnational level, the range is 18% compared to 14% in the United States. This suggests that, at least for economic growth, the differences in the range of variation between Canada and the United States may help explain much of the differing impact of economic freedom. However, since the range of variation itself,

Table 4: Growth in Economic Freedom and Growth in Per-Capita GDP

Regressions at All-Government Level (ALLG)　Regressions at Subnational Level (SUBN)

Dependent Variable: Growth in Per Capita GDP (1994-2000)　Dependent Variable: Growth in Per Capita GDP (1994-2000)
Method: Pooled Least Squares
Sample: 1994-2000

Canada

Total panel (balanced) observations: 70

Variable	Coefficient	Std. Error	t-Statistic	Prob.	Variable	Coefficient	Std. Error	t-Statistic	Prob.
HGG	0.00	0.06	0.07	0.94	HGG	0.04	0.07	0.53	0.60
POPG	0.15	0.78	0.19	0.85	POPG	0.52	0.91	0.57	0.57
ALLGG	0.52	0.10	5.47	0.00	SUBNG	0.40	0.11	3.70	0.00

Adjusted R²: 0.35　　Adjusted R²: 0.21

United States

Total panel (balanced) observations: 350

Variable	Coefficient	Std. Error	t-Statistic	Prob.	Variable	Coefficient	Std. Error	t-Statistic	Prob.
HGG	0.00	0.01	-0.04	0.97	HGG	0.01	0.02	0.54	0.59
POPG	-0.07	0.28	-0.24	0.81	POPG	0.10	0.35	0.28	0.78
ALLGG	1.00	0.06	16.48	0.00	SUBNG	0.48	0.06	8.04	0.00

Adjusted R²: 0.51　　Adjusted R²: 0.24

Notes
HGG is growth in the number of high school graduates per 10,000 people (25 years and older) from 1994 to 2000;
POPG is growth in population from 1994 to 2000;
ALLGG is growth in economic freedom at an all-government level from 1994 to 2000;
SUBNG is growth in economic freedom at a subnational level from 1994 to 2000.

obviously, does not determine the size of the coefficient, more research is required here to examine differences between Canada and the United States.

Sensitivity Analysis

In order to determine the stability of the regression results in the Tables 3 and 4, further testing was done using moving averages rather than annual data. These results can be found below. Further sensitivity analysis, including tests using Canadian dollars and tests using different income tax calculations, can be found on www.freetheworld.com.

The use of moving averages (reported in Tables 5 and 6) is important. Annual data in regression analysis may lead to misleading results because, depending on the period of study, business cycles may inflate or deflate the estimated coefficients. The data used in the regression analyses in Tables 5 and 6 are smoothed out through use of a moving average, minimizing the impact of business cycles. The variables are the same as before. Significance levels remain high except for some of the longer moving averages for Canadian data. The results are interesting in themselves in that they throw further light on the impact of fiscal federalism and the impact of economic freedom over time.

Levels

The regression results in Table 5 indicate that the level of economic freedom has a strong impact on per-capita GDP regardless of period used for calculating the moving averages. The significance of the coefficient stays high, regardless of the number of periods in the moving average, at both subnational and all-government levels. The results are also consistent with the earlier finding that the level of economic freedom has a stronger impact on US states than on the Canadian provinces.

For US states, the longer the time period covered by the moving average, the greater the impact of economic freedom. This is likely because the impact of economic freedom is not instantaneous and, therefore, within reasonable limits the longer the period under consideration, the greater the impact of economic freedom.[3] As well, gains in economic growth, like savings, compound over time and, thus, longer time periods show larger effects.

Yet, this pattern—a positive correlation between the coefficient on economic freedom and the length of time over which it is calculated—is exactly reversed for the Canadian data at both the all-government level and subnational levels. This strongly suggests that fiscal federalism, by transferring funds from provinces that have a high degree of economic freedom to those with less economic freedom and effectively increasing the tax burden in freer provinces, mutes the effect of economic freedom over time. In other words, fiscal federalism not only imposes an immediate penalty upon relatively free provinces in comparison with US states, but a penalty that becomes greater over time. Thus, economic freedom has a weaker impact in Canada than in the United States and the gap grows over time.

Finally, the pattern differentiating all-government testing from subnational testing remains consistent regardless of period. For both Canada and the United States, the impact of economic freedom at the all-government level is greater than the impact at the subnational level regardless of time period.

Growth

The regression results in Table 6 indicate that the estimated coefficients on the growth in economic freedom using moving average data are very similar to the regression results using annual data.

The coefficient on economic freedom in US testing appears to have a slight upward tendency but not as pronounced as in the tests on levels. This is to be expected since the compounding effects of economic freedom will affect only levels and not growth rates, just as compounding of interest affects only the sum being saved and not the interest rate, itself. For Canada, there is no clear relationship between the size of the coefficient and the length of the moving average.

Additional sensitivity tests were run using data back to 1981 using four-year time periods. In other words, data for 1981, 1985, 1989, 1993 and 1997 were used. Here again the results in Tables 7 and 8 are consistent with what has already been found.

For the US states in particular, all the results—all-government and subnational—are highly similar to both the results reported in the main body of the text and with the rolling average testing and consistent with the idea that economic freedom has a greater impact the longer the time period under consideration. This is true, with the provisos noted above about compounding, for both the growth and the level regressions.

Table 5: Level of Economic Freedom and Per-Capita GDP: Moving Averages

Dependent Variable: Real Per Capita GDP (1993-2000)

Method: Pooled Least Squares

	2-period backward moving average		3-period backward moving average		4-period backward moving average		5-period backward moving average	
Canada at an All-Government Level								
Total panel (balanced) observations:	70		60		50		40	
Variable	Coefficient	t-Statistic	Coefficient	t-Statistic	Coefficient	t-Statistic	Coefficient	t-Statistic
HG	2.89	0.38	0.69	0.08	0.23	0.02	-2.57	-0.18
ALLG	2372.70	5.76	2243.23	5.09	2070.46	3.56	1894.18	2.38
	Adjusted R^2: 0.99		Adjusted R^2: 0.99		Adjusted R^2: 1.00		Adjusted R^2: 1.00	
Canada at a Subnational Level								
Total panel (balanced) observations:	70		60		50		40	
Variable	Coefficient	t-Statistic	Coefficient	t-Statistic	Coefficient	t-Statistic	Coefficient	t-Statistic
HG	-7.21	-0.99	-9.59	-1.27	-10.46	-1.17	-15.53	-1.35
SUBN	1786.46	4.99	1678.96	4.80	1521.59	3.57	1334.20	2.30
	Adjusted R^2: 0.99		Adjusted R^2: 0.99		Adjusted R^2: 1.00		Adjusted R^2: 1.00	
United States at an All-Government Level								
Total panel (balanced) observations:	350		300		250		200	
Variable	Coefficient	t-Statistic	Coefficient	t-Statistic	Coefficient	t-Statistic	Coefficient	t-Statistic
HG	-2.64	-0.74	-3.58	-0.79	-3.32	-0.64	-3.78	-0.67
ALLG	7493.55	18.79	7701.84	17.62	7732.11	15.33	7926.67	13.14
	Adjusted R^2: 0.99		Adjusted R^2: 0.99		Adjusted R^2: 0.99		Adjusted R^2: 1.00	
United States at a Subnational Level								
Total panel (balanced) observations:	350		300		250		200	
Variable	Coefficient	t-Statistic	Coefficient	t-Statistic	Coefficient	t-Statistic	Coefficient	t-Statistic
HG	-0.94	-0.20	-2.31	-0.39	-2.37	-0.36	-1.99	-0.28
SUBN	3450.49	9.98	3513.94	9.28	3491.28	8.19	3531.99	6.93
	Adjusted R^2: 0.98		Adjusted R^2: 0.99		Adjusted R^2: 0.99		Adjusted R^2: 0.99	

Notes

HG is the number of high school graduates per 10,000 people (25 years and older) from 1993 to 2000;

ALLG is an economic freedom index at an all-government level from 1993 to 2000;

SUBN is an economic freedom index at a subnational level from 1993 to 2000.

Table 6: Growth in Economic Freedom and Growth in Per-Capita GDP: Moving Averages

Dependent Variable: Growth in Per Capita GDP (1994-2000)

Method: Pooled Least Squares

	2-period backward moving average		3-period backward moving average		4-period backward moving average		5-period backward moving average	
Canada at an All-Government Level								
Total panel (balanced) observations:	60		50		40		30	
HGG	0.01	0.14	0.02	0.31	0.03	0.43	0.05	0.35
POPG	1.13	1.88	1.42	2.88	1.81	3.30	2.27	2.17
ALLGG	0.62	7.23	0.64	8.05	0.68	6.38	0.47	1.71
	Adjusted R²: 0.54		Adjusted R²: 0.68		Adjusted R²: 0.72		Adjusted R²: 0.65	
Canada at a Subnational Level								
Total panel (balanced) observations:	60		50		40		30	
HGG	0.02	0.21	0.02	0.27	-0.05	-0.65	-0.03	-0.25
POPG	1.55	2.16	1.93	3.58	2.11	3.72	1.85	1.77
SUBNG	0.55	5.24	0.61	7.35	0.57	6.29	0.20	1.05
	Adjusted R²: 0.39		Adjusted R²: 0.64		Adjusted R²: 0.72		Adjusted R²: 0.61	
United States at an All-Government Level								
Total panel (balanced) observations:	300		250		200		150	
HGG	0.01	0.96	0.01	0.47	0.01	0.93	0.01	0.67
POPG	-0.02	-0.10	0.08	0.42	0.01	0.03	0.04	0.14
ALLGG	1.06	18.00	1.09	17.29	1.07	13.83	1.13	9.41
	Adjusted R²: 0.70		Adjusted R²: 0.81		Adjusted R²: 0.87		Adjusted R²: 0.91	
United States at a Subnational Level								
Total panel (balanced) observations:	300		250		200		150	
HGG	0.02	1.08	0.01	0.64	0.01	0.72	0.02	0.81
POPG	0.01	0.02	0.23	0.90	0.17	0.62	0.15	0.43
SUBNG	0.52	9.34	0.58	9.24	0.56	7.33	0.47	5.18
	Adjusted R²: 0.48		Adjusted R²: 0.67		Adjusted R²: 0.79		Adjusted R²: 0.86	

Notes

HGG is growth in the number of high school graduates per 10,000 people (25 years and older) from 1994 to 2000;

POPG is growth in population from 1994 to 2000;

ALLGG is growth in economic freedom at an all-government level from 1994 to 2000;

SUBNG is growth in economic freedom at a subnational level from 1994 to 2000.

Table 7: Level of Economic Freedom and Per-Capita GDP—Four-Year Periods

Regressions at All-Government Level					Regressions at Subnational Level				
Dependent Variable: Real Per Capita GDP					Dependent Variable: Real Per Capita GDP				
Method: Pooled Least Squares					Method: Pooled Least Squares				
Sample: 1981, 1985, 1989, 1993, 1997					Sample: 1981, 1985, 1989, 1993, 1997				

Canada

Total panel (balanced) observations: 50					Total panel (balanced) observations: 50				
Variable	Coefficient	Std. Error	t-Statistic	Prob.	Variable	Coefficient	Std. Error	t-Statistic	Prob.
HG	−14.65	19.96	−0.73	0.47	HG	−14.69	20.36	−0.72	0.48
ALLG	1335.48	527.15	2.53	0.02	SUBN	1461.78	666.16	2.19	0.03
		Adjusted R^2: 0.90					Adjusted R^2: 0.90		

United States

Total panel (balanced) observations: 250					Total panel (balanced) observations: 250				
Variable	Coefficient	Std. Error	t-Statistic	Prob.	Variable	Coefficient	Std. Error	t-Statistic	Prob.
HG	−28.11	13.16	−2.14	0.03	HG	−33.47	14.64	−2.29	0.02
ALLG	9659.43	672.63	14.36	0.00	SUBN	7242.05	641.76	11.28	0.00
		Adjusted R^2: 0.88					Adjusted R^2: 0.85		

Notes

HG is the number of high school graduates per 10,000 people (25 years and older) from 1993 to 2000;

ALLG is an economic freedom index at an all-government level from 1993 to 2000;

SUBN is an economic freedom index at a subnational level from 1993 to 2000.

Table 8: Growth in Economic Freedom and Growth in Per-Capita GDP—Four-Year Periods

Regressions at All-Government Level					Regressions at Subnational Level				
Dependent Variable: Growth in Per Capita GDP					Dependent Variable: Growth in Per Capita GDP				
Method: Pooled Least Squares					Method: Pooled Least Squares				
Sample: 1985, 1989, 1993, 1997					Sample: 1985, 1989, 1993, 1997				

Canada

Total panel (balanced) observations: 40					Total panel (balanced) observations: 40				
Variable	Coefficient	Std. Error	t-Statistic	Prob.	Variable	Coefficient	Std. Error	t-Statistic	Prob.
HGG	0.13	0.14	0.91	0.37	HGG	0.33	0.15	2.17	0.05
POPG	1.45	0.77	1.88	0.07	POPG	1.60	0.78	2.07	0.00
ALLGG	0.36	0.09	4.10	0.00	SUBNG	0.72	0.17	4.10	0.00
		Adjusted R^2: 0.32					Adjusted R^2: 0.32		

United States

Total panel (balanced) observations: 200					Total panel (balanced) observations: 200				
Variable	Coefficient	Std. Error	t-Statistic	Prob.	Variable	Coefficient	Std. Error	t-Statistic	Prob.
HGG	0.08	0.05	1.62	0.11	HGG	0.16	0.05	3.12	0.01
POPG	0.18	0.16	1.11	0.27	POPG	0.46	0.17	2.80	0.00
ALLGG	1.00	0.08	12.05	0.00	SUBNG	0.72	0.07	10.51	0.00
		Adjusted R^2: 0.67					Adjusted R^2: 0.63		

Notes

HGG is growth in the number of high school graduates per 10,000 people (25 years and older) from 1994 to 2000;

POPG is growth in population from 1994 to 2000;

ALLGG is growth in economic freedom at an all-government level from 1994 to 2000;

SUBNG is growth in economic freedom at a subnational level from 1994 to 2000.

The Canadian results are also consistent with earlier results and with comments about fiscal federalism. In particular, the coefficient on economic freedom again seems typically to be reduced by longer time periods, for both levels and growth rates. The coefficient on growth in economic freedom in the subnational regression is larger in Table 8, using four-year periods, than in Table 4, using annual data, suggesting the need for further investigation. It may simply be, as noted above, that the muting effects of fiscal federalism are smaller at the subnational level than at the all-government level, allowing the advantages of economic freedom over time to be more apparent in subnational testing.

The Importance of Economic Freedom

This paper has focused on the measurement of economic freedom and on empirical testing of the impact of economic freedom. However, the reader may wonder why economic freedom is so clearly related to growth and prosperity, a finding not just of this paper but also of many other empirical explorations of economic freedom.

In many ways, this debate goes back to the beginnings of modern economics when Adam Smith famously argued that each of us, freely pursuing our own ends, create the wealth of nations and of the individual citizens. However, the twentieth century was much consumed by a debate about whether planned or free economies produce the best outcomes. The results of the experiments of the twentieth century should be clear. Free economies produced the greatest prosperity in human history for their citizens. Even poverty in these economically free nations would have been considered luxury in unfree economies. This lesson was reinforced by the collapse of centrally planned states and, following this, the consistent refusal of their citizens to return to central planning, regardless of the hardships on the road to freedom. Among developing nations, those that adopted the centrally planned model have only produced lives of misery for their citizens. Those that adopted the economics of competitive markets have begun to share with their citizens the prosperity of advanced market economies.

While these comparisons are extreme examples, from opposite ends of the economic freedom spectrum, a considerable body of research shows the relationship between prosperity and economic freedom holds in narrower ranges of the spectrum. While sophisticated econometric testing backs up this relationship, examples are also interesting. So, for example taking two peripheral European nations, the relatively free Ireland does much better than the relatively unfree Greece. In the United States, the relatively free Georgia does much better than the relatively unfree West Virginia. In Canada, an unfree Quebec does much worse than its freer neighbour, Ontario. As with anything in the real world, exceptions can be found, but overall the strength of the statistical fit of this relationship is remarkable.

While this is hardly the place to review several centuries of economic debate, the mechanics of economic freedom are easy to understand. Any transaction freely entered into must benefit both parties. Any transaction, which does not benefit both parties, would be rejected by the party that would come up short. This has consequences throughout the economy. Consumers who are free to choose will only be attracted by superior quality and price. A producer must constantly improve its price and quality to meet customer demands or customers will not freely enter into transactions with the producer. Many billions of mutually beneficial transactions occur every day, powering the dynamic that spurs increased productivity and wealth throughout the economy.

Restrictions on freedom prevent people from making mutually beneficial transactions. Such free transactions are replaced by government action. This is marked by coercion, in collecting taxes, and lack of choice, in accepting services. Instead of gains for both parties arising from each transaction, citizens must pay whatever bill is demanded in taxes and accept whatever service is offered in return. Moreover, while the incentives of producers in a free market revolve around providing superior goods and services in order to attract consumers, the public sector faces no such incentives. Instead, as public-choice theory reveals, incentives in the public sector often focus on rewarding interest groups, seeking political advantage, or even penalizing unpopular groups. This is far different from mutually beneficial exchange although, as noted earlier, government does have essential protective and productive functions.

In some ways it is surprising the debate still rages because the evidence and theory favouring economic freedom match intuition. Intuitively it makes sense that the drive and ingenuity of all citizens, harnessed to better outcomes through the mechanism of mutually beneficial exchange, will surely do better for themselves than will a small coterie of government planners, who hardly have knowledge of everyone's values and who, being human, are likely to consider their own well-being and the constituencies they must please when making decisions for all of us.

Conclusion

The worldwide evidence on economic freedom suggests that the Canadian provinces are poorly positioned to take advantage of economic opportunity. The provinces are clustered near the bottom of the rankings in all three areas, indicating that their governments have consumed and transferred more resources, imposed higher tax rates, and created more rigid labor markets than the governments of US states.

The regression analyses indicate that growth in economic freedom and the level of economic freedom have a significant impact on the growth in per-capita GDP and the level of per-capita GDP. Since Canadian provinces have relatively low levels of economic freedom, Canadians are likely to continue to experience lower standards of living relative to American states. Only two provinces, Alberta and Ontario, have high levels of economic freedom in the Canadian context, and their residents have seen the benefits of this.

Notes

1 As already mentioned, the omission of the investment variable does not seriously affect the coefficients on economic freedom. We tested the impact of the exclusion of the investment variable from the model of Mankiw, Romer, and Weil (1992), enhanced by an economic freedom variable. The exclusion does not change the estimated coefficients on economic freedom nor their standard errors significantly.

2 Stability testing reveals that regression results in Tables 3 and 4 are not sensitive to the method of estimation or to the model specification. The results change little when random effects are used to estimate the coefficients or when the high-school variable (our proxy for human capital) or the population-growth variable is excluded from the model. Note that the covariance matrix of the estimated standard errors is virtually identical to the heteroscedasticity consistent White matrix. Exclusion of the outliers, Alberta and Alaska, from Table 3 and Newfoundland, Alberta, British Columbia, Alaska, and Hawaii from Table 4 does not change the estimated coefficients on economic freedom or their standard errors significantly.

3 The qualification "reasonable limits" is included since, over too long a period, increases and decreases in economic freedom would tend to cancel out, at least partly, in individual jurisdictions, reducing the measured impact.

Appendix A: The Economic Health of the Provinces and States

Canada

Alberta

For a Canadian province, Alberta had high levels of economic freedom at the opening of the 1980s. However, through the 1980s and early 1990s, Alberta's policy mix shifted and the level of economic freedom declined. The province's economy weakened and unemployment rose to a national level, sometimes exceeding national rate of unemployment. After a dozen years of decline, Alberta's economic freedom began to grow in 1994. At the same time, the gap between per-capita GDP in Alberta and the rest of Canada, which had been shrinking, once again started to grow in Alberta's favour and Alberta's unemployment fell to significantly below the national average. In Area 1: Size of Government, which examines government spending, at the all-government level, Alberta typically scores highly because it has a very low level of federal expenditures but ranks lower on the taxation variable, because of the high level of federal taxation. The opposite pattern holds in the subnational index, spending scores are lower than taxation scores.

British Columbia

In the all-government index, British Columbia maintained third spot among the provinces in economic freedom throughout the 1990s. However, its ranking dropped on the subnational index from 52nd spot in 1993 to 56th in 2000. British Columbia's relative affluence also declined sharply over the period, from 15% above the national average in 1993 to a virtual tie with the national average in 2000. Even though migration to British Columbia fell off sharply through the 1990s, the unemployment rate rose relative to the national average. In 1993, British Columbia's unemployment rate was 1.7 percentage points below the national average. By 2000, the province's unemployment rate was 0.4 percentage points above the national average.

Manitoba

Manitoba significantly reduced its economic freedom in both indexes from 1981 to the early 1990s. Economic freedom recovered somewhat from the mid-1990s onward but Manitoba's score in 2000 was significantly below its score in 1981 on both indexes. Over the period, Manitoba's per-capita GDP fell from just above the national average to about $1,500 below. However, Manitoba's unemployment rate remained below the national average throughout the period, though this may be partially due to significant emigration from the middle of the 1980s onward. Manitoba's downward trend in economic freedom is more or less consistently reflected across the subindexes.

New Brunswick

New Brunswick had the second strongest gains in economic freedom of all provinces over the full period. Gains were reflected in both indexes, though between 1989 and 1993 New Brunswick did suffer some declines in economic freedom. After 1993, gains were consistent and large. However, because its score was initially so low, New Brunswick's score at the end of the period remained slightly below the Canadian average in both indexes. Nonetheless, just as New Brunswick significantly closed the economic-freedom gap with other provinces over the period, it also closed the income gap, rising from less than 70% of average provincial per-capita GDP in 1981 to over 80% in 2000. This progress stalled after 1995, the highwater mark of New Brunswick's economic freedom score relative to other Canadian provinces. New Brunswick's unemployment rate, relative to the rest of Canada, fluctuated over the period. However, given first, the various perverse incentives in Canada's Employment Insurance system, which in Atlantic Canada operates under rules that are, in effect, different from those used in the rest of the nation, and, second, attempts over the period to reform the system that resulted in a number of changes and reverses, it is difficult to know what to make of posted unemployment rates in Atlantic Canada. An idea of the perverse incentives is found in the fact that the number of people officially unemployed in Atlantic Canada has been typically smaller than the number of people collecting employment insurance.

Newfoundland

Newfoundland began the period close to the bottom of the heap in both indexes and remained there until 1998. Although Newfoundland's score improved over the 1990s, it was only keeping pace with improvements in other provinces. However, between 1998 and 2000, Newfoundland made substantive improvements and its ranking rose to a middling position among the provinces. Since the mid-1980s, Newfoundland's unemployment has been roughly double the Canadian average. However, Newfoundland rapidly gained on the rest of Canada in per-capita GDP at the end of the 1990s. But, Newfoundland's economy is small and undiversified. Thus, if key sectors suffer external shocks, it becomes difficult to disentangle general economic trends from the impact of these shocks. Both the fishing and oil industries are sensitive to exogenous shocks such as price swings and resource changes, due to exploration in the petrochemical industry and fish stocks in the fishing sector.

Nova Scotia

Scotia had the largest gains in economic freedom among Canadian provinces. Nova Scotia's scoring and ranking improved substantially in both indexes. It began the period dead last in the all-government index and rose to become the fourth highest ranked province. In the subnational index, it rose from third last to third best among the provinces. However, Nova Scotia's climb in the rankings ended in 1993. It had the same relative ranking in 2000. Nova Scotia's per-capita GDP also climbed significantly relative to the national average until 1993 and has since stagnated compared to the Canadian average. Nova Scotia's unemployment rate remained largely stable against the Canadian average. Over the full period, it was typically about 2 percentage points above the Canadian average.

Ontario

Between 1989 and 1993, Ontario's economic freedom dropped dramatically. This followed an earlier, though less dramatic decline, through the 1980s. In 1981, Ontario had higher levels of economic freedom than at least some states in both indexes. By 1993, it had fallen below all states in the all-government index and it remained behind Alberta among Canadian provinces. In the subnational index, it rated below three provinces, Alberta, British Columbia, and Nova Scotia in 1993. Through the rest of the 1990s, Ontario's score climbed in both indexes. Ontario's per-capita GDP declined significantly against the Canadian average between 1989 and 1993 but has remained largely stable since. Ontario's unemployment rate, which had been 2.4 percentage points below the Canadian average in 1989, was only 0.5 percentage points below the Canadian average by 1993. By the end of the 1990s, the unemployment gap had more than doubled in Ontario's favour, with Ontario posting an unemployment rate that was slightly more than 1.0 percentage points below the Canadian average.

Prince Edward Island

Prince Edward Island (PEI) and Quebec are the worst performing provinces. Prince Edward Island began the period with a score close to the bottom among Canadian provinces in both indexes. It ended the period dead last in the all-government index and second last in the subnational index. Prince Edward Island also had poor scores in all the sub-indexes. Since it fell into the bottom rankings in the late 1980s, its unemployment rate has ranged between 60% and 90% higher than the national rate. Since the 1980s, PEI's per-capita GDP has remained fairly constant at about 80% of the Canadian average, give or take a couple of percentage points.

Quebec

In every year, Quebec has scored dead last in economic freedom in the subnational index. It has always been close to the bottom of the all-government index and, since 1995, has been second or third last in that index. Throughout the full period, Quebec's unemployment rate has remained remarkably consistent at about two percentage points above the Canadian average. However, in the late 1980s and early 1990s, Quebec's per-capita GDP rose slightly relative to the rest of Canada, bringing its per-capita GDP up to the national average. Since then, Quebec's per-capita GDP declined relative to the Canadian average and, in 2000, was about 2 percentage points below the Canadian average.

Saskatchewan

Saskatchewan has been consistently in the middle of the Canadian ranks through the full period under examination, though its relative ranking declined somewhat towards the middle of the 1990s. Saskatchewan, like Manitoba but unlike the eastern "have-not" provinces, has had an unemployment rate that has been consistently below the Canadian average, though the gap has begun to shrink. Until 1996, Saskatchewan's unemployment rate was consistently about 3 percentage points lower than the Canadian average. By 2000, that gap had shrunk to 2 percentage points.

The United States

Alabama

Alabama ranked 15th overall in terms of economic freedom at the all-government level, and was 11th in the subnational index. Its comparatively high overall ranking came in part because of its showing in labor market freedom—it was the highest ranked state or province in both all-government and state and local (subnational) in 2000. It placed well in takings and discriminatory taxation (10th state and local, 15th all-government). Only a handful of states had a lower effective state and local tax burden. Alabama has a relatively low general sales and use tax, 4%, and one of the lowest cigarette taxes in the country, 16.5¢ per pack. Alabama would have placed higher overall had it not been for its rating in the size of government category, where it was ranked 46th all-government and 39th state and local.

Alaska

Alaska ranked 45th overall when compared to other states and provinces in the all-government rankings, and 50th at the state and local group. While it fared comparatively well in takings and discriminatory taxation (8th all-government, 17th state and local—with no general sales and use tax, an extremely

low 8¢ gasoline tax and the lowest effective state and local tax burden of the 50 states), it was pulled down by the other measurements. Alaska was 35th in labor market freedom in the all-government category and 30th in state and local. It was 55th in the broad grouping when it came to size of government, and 60th in the subnational category—dead last among all states and provinces.

Arizona

Arizona ranks 9th overall in the all-government listings and 7th in the state and local ratings, thanks to a fairly consistent performance in all three categories. Its best showing came in labor market freedom where it was 4th in all-government and 3rd in state and local comparisons. While it placed 24th in the size of government in the all-government measurement it jumped to 11th in the state and local list. Arizona improved its performance in takings and discriminatory taxation from the previous year in the all-government group where it was ranked 20th, and ranked 17th state and local in 2000. It is about in the middle of the pack in terms of effective state and local tax burden (28th) and a 5% general sales and use tax.

Arkansas

Arkansas placed 45th overall in the all-government category and slightly higher—39th—in the state and local comparisons. Far and away its best showing was in state and local size of government, where it ranked 19th, as compared to 38th in the all-government rankings. Otherwise, the state fell into the second half on the other two measurements: 37th in all-government and 36th in state and local takings and taxation; and, despite marginal improvement over the previous year, 49th in both categories for labor market freedom. Its effective state and local tax burden of 10.2% places it in about the middle of the pack

California

California ranked 20th overall in terms of economic freedom at the all-government level but ranked 36th when its state and local numbers were compared with other states and provinces. This disparity reflects all three areas of measurement. The state ranked relatively high (14th) in terms of government size at the all-government level but fared worse at the state and local level, dropping to 34th. The state and local ranking also suffered when compared with all-government numbers in takings and discriminatory taxation: 41st for the former, and 26th for the latter. Its ratings for labor market freedom showed marginal improvement from 1999, and placed it in the middle of the pack, ranking 26th for all-government and 27th for state and local. Only seven states have a higher general sales and use tax than California's 6%. Its total state and local tax burden is just above the national average at 10.3%.

Colorado

Colorado is one of the leading states in terms of economic freedom, placing 2nd in all-government overall and 3rd in state and local. With one exception—the state and local measurement for takings and taxation, where it ranked 14th—the state was in the top five in all areas. For size of government, it ranked 5th in the all-government list and 3rd in state and local. It improved slightly in labor market freedom, finishing 2nd in both rankings. In all-government takings and taxation, Colorado ranked 4th. The state's general use and sales tax, at 2.9%, is the lowest in the country for those states that have one. Only four states have a lower effective state and local tax burden. And, Coloradoans can celebrate their good fortune cheaply: only three states have a lower tax on beer.

Connecticut

Connecticut places 9th overall in the all-government ratings and 14th in state and local. Far and away its best measure of economic freedom is in labor market freedom, where it placed 4th in the all-government area and 6th in state and local. Otherwise, the state was ranked 12th and 19th for all-government and state and local respectively in size of government, and 32nd and 23rd for takings and discriminatory taxation. Its general sales and use tax is at the high end at 6%. Its gasoline tax of 25¢ per gallon is tied for 4th highest in the country. Its effective state and local tax burden is the 11th highest but its total tax burden, 36.7%, is top in the country.

Delaware

Delaware sets the standard for economic freedom in the United States, placing 1st overall in both the all-government and state and local rankings. In terms

of government size, it was rated 1st in all-government and 4th in the state and local comparison. A substantial improvement in takings and taxation in the state and local category earned it a 1st place there, matching its number-one standing in all-government. Its labor market freedom rankings were only slightly lower: 4th in all-government, 6th in state and local. Delaware has no general sales and use tax. Its effective state and local tax burden is about in the middle of state rankings at 27th.

Florida

Florida ranked considerably higher overall in the state and local comparisons than in the all-government group, 17th as opposed to 29th. That pattern repeats itself in two of the three measurements. The state's size of government ranking is 38th in all-government (showing a marginal improvement from the previous year) and 18th in state and local; for takings and taxation the relative rankings are 43rd and 24th. Florida's best showing came in labor market freedom, where it placed 11th in both measurements. Its effective state and local tax burden of 9.3% ranks it 43rd among the states. Its general sales and use tax is at the high end (6%) but gasoline tax of 4¢ per gallon is the lowest in the country.

Georgia

Georgia has solid ratings on most measures of economic freedom, placing 5th overall in the all-government group and 7th in state and local. Its best ratings are for size of government: 2nd state and local, and 5th in all-government, and the all-government ranking for takings and taxation, 4th. It came in 17th in that category in subnational. Georgia slowed slight improvement in labor market freedom over the previous year, ranking 20th in all-government and 19th state and local. Its general sales and use tax is at the low end of states that have it (4%) and its gasoline tax is the second lowest in the country at 7.5¢. At 10.2% its effective state and local tax burden is exactly in the middle of the pack at 25th.

Hawaii

Hawaii only managed to crack the top 30 on one measurement. Overall it ranked 39th in all-government and 36th in state and local. For size of government, it ranks 41st in all-government and 39th state and local. The takings and taxation numbers put it at 37th for all government and 47th for state and local (and its effective state and local tax burden is the 4th highest in the country at 11.6%). Only in labor market freedom, state and local, did it make it to 24th (and 32nd for all-government). Its general sales and use tax is 4%.

Idaho

Almost all of Idaho rankings fall in a relatively narrow range. Its overall rating for all-government is 35th and for state and local 42nd. Size of government ratings put it at 31st for all-government and 34th for state and local. Its labor market freedom rankings are the same for both categories at 37th. Idaho shows the widest disparity in takings and taxation, ranking 30th in all-government but 45th for state and local, after both improved a bit over the previous year. At 25¢ per gallon, its gasoline tax is higher than most other states. The effective state and local tax burden is 10.5%, placing it 17th among the states.

Illinois

Except for its ratings on labor market freedom, Illinois places solidly at the bottom of the top 3rd of the rankings. In overall all-government, it finishes 14th, and in state and local 17th. In terms of size of government, it rates 4th in the all-government index and 14th in the subnational index, and for takings and taxation it ranks 15th for all-government and 14th for state and local. Its overall ratings are pulled down somewhat—despite a small improvement over the previous year—in labor market freedom, finishing in the mid-20s in both indexes. Illinois has one of the nation's highest general sales and use tax rates at 6.25%, and a fairly high spirits tax at $4.50 per gallon. Its effective state and local tax burden places it 31st among the states at 10%, but its total tax burden of 32.8% ranks it 9th.

Indiana

Indiana has a high rating for economic freedom, placing 4th in the overall rankings for both all-government and state and local. Its strengths are takings and taxation (8th all-government and 4th state and local) and labor market freedom (8th and 6th). It stumbles only somewhat on size of government, dropping to 17th all-government and 8th state and local. At 9.9%, Indiana

ranks 34th in effective state and local tax burdens. Its gasoline tax at 15¢ per gallon is toward the low end of the scale.

Iowa

Iowa is stuck in the middle both geographically and numerically, pulling down a 39th overall ranking for all-governments and a 34th for state and local. Its showings in two of the three categories correspond: a 24th all-government and a 28th state and local for size of government and a 37th all-government and a 27th state and local for taxation. Iowa's low point, however, comes from labor market freedom. Despite a marginal improvement from the previous year, it only ranked 44th in all-government and 47th state and local. Indiana beat most states on its gasoline tax at 15¢ per gallon, and only came in as the 34th most burdensome state in terms of effective state and local taxes at 9.9%.

Kansas

Kansas is another state in which economic freedom is neither enshrined nor defeated. It ranked 26th in all-government overall and 21st in state and local. Its best showing was in size of government, state and local, where it rated 14th (all-government was 24th), after which there was almost no diversion between the two measurements. Takings and taxation finished 32nd in all-government and 31st in subnational, and labor market freedom 22nd by both measurements. Kansas ranks 21st in effective state and local tax burden and 23rd in total tax burden.

Kentucky

Kentucky rates 33rd overall in the all-government list and 28th in the state and local, which more or less sums up its record since 1981: fluctuating in the 20s and 30s on both the indexes. Its size of government ratings are 34th and 21st respectively, while in the takings and discriminatory taxation measurement, it finished 15th and 24th. Kentucky's weakest performance was in labor market freedom: 35th all-government and 37th state and local. The effective state and local tax burden is the 18th highest at 10.5%. At least sin isn't heavily taxed: only Virginia beats its 3¢ tax per pack of cigarettes, and the tax on beer of 8¢ is among the country's lowest. Gasoline is also taxed gently at 15¢ per gallon.

Louisiana

Louisiana came out 15th overall in all-government and 14th state and local. Its best showings for economic freedom came in takings and taxation (12th in all-government and 16th state and local) and labor market freedom (11th all-government and 13th state and local). Louisiana's overall ranking was dragged down somewhat by its numbers on size of government: 33rd all-government and 21st state and local. The state's general sales and use tax is at the low end at 4% and—perhaps due to the weight New Orleans throws around—the state's tax on table wine is the lowest in the country at 11¢ per gallon. That's *gallon*.

Maine

If you're a detective looking for clues to find economic freedom, you don't need to schedule time investigating Maine. Overall the state ranks 49th all-government and 47th state and local. On takings and taxation, it is actually beaten by a couple of the woeful Canadian provinces, finishing 51st among states and provinces all-government and 55th state and local. The record is little better on size of government (46th all-government, 42nd state and local) and labor market freedom, which, despite a marginal improvement from the previous year, still ranks 46th in both measurements. It has the highest effective state and local tax burden in the United States at 12.8%.

Maryland

Maryland's record on economic freedom is lackluster on most counts. The state finished 41st overall in the all-government measurement and 25th in the state and local. Its best showing came in the state and local rankings for takings and taxation where it placed 10th; it was 23rd in all-government. Maryland's rankings for size of government were 41st in all-government and 21st in state and local. The labor market freedom rankings were below average at 47th for all-government and 37th state and local. There are a couple of bright spots: Maryland's effective state and local tax burden is 37th out of the 50 states at 9.7%, and its tax on beer is among the nation's lowest at 9¢.

Massachusetts

Massachusetts doesn't rate spectacularly high in any single measurement but its general disposition to eco-nomic freedom places it 5th overall in all-government and 7th in state and local. In size of government, it showed marginal improvement in the all-government ratings and placed 10th; it was 11th in state and local. Again, a slight improvement in labor market freedom earned it 17th and 16th rankings, respectively. Easily its best marks came in takings and taxation, 8th in all-government and 4th state and local. Massachusetts is 39th out of the states in effective state and local tax burden at 9.5%.

Michigan

Michigan's labor market freedom numbers helped pull up its overall rankings somewhat (it placed 20th overall in all-government and 23rd in state and local). The labor ratings placed in 16th in both categories. Otherwise, the state was 32nd in takings and discriminatory taxation in the all-government index and 24th in the state and local index; and 22nd and 30th, respectively, in size of government. Its general sales and use tax was comparatively high at 6%, and at 10.7% its effective state and local tax burden is 14th highest among the states. Smokers only pay higher cigarette taxes in 7 other states (75¢).

Minnesota

Minnesota tied Michigan for 20th place in the all-government overall rankings and 31st in state and local measurements of economic freedom. A slight improvement in size of government in the all-government area landed it a 5th place spot in those rankings, which it placed 27th in state and local. Otherwise, its ratings were farther back in the pack: for all-government and state and local, Minnesota was 32nd and 41st respectively in takings and taxation and 24th and 25th in labor market freedom. Its general sales and use tax was on the high end at 6.5%, and the effective state and local tax burden is the country's 5th highest at 11.3%.

Mississippi

Mississippi's competitive scores in labor market freedom were about the only bright spot for the state that placed 41st overall in the all-government rankings and 28th in state and local. Its respective rankings for labor were 11th and 13th. Otherwise, economic freedom takes a beating. A slight worsening from the previous year's figures made it 51st among the states and provinces in size of government in the all-government rankings and 33rd in state and local. It finished 40th and 45th respectively in takings and discriminatory taxation. Its 7% general sales and use tax ties Rhode Island for the highest in the nation; at 10.7% its effective state and local tax burden is the country's 15th highest.

Missouri

Missouri ranks 15th overall in the all-government rankings and 7th in state and local, with respectable scores in both takings and discriminatory taxation (12th and 7th, respectively) and labor market freedom (17th and 16th). It fairs worse in the all-government measurement for size of government, coming in 32nd, although in the state and local rankings it placed 11th. It has a relative low general sales and use tax, among the states that charge one, at 4.225% and tipplers enjoy the nation's second-lowest tax on beer (6¢) and one of the lowest table wine taxes (30¢). In the rankings where citizens want their state to finish far down the line, effective state and local tax burden, Missouri is 38th at 9.7%.

Montana

Montana ranked 50th overall in the all-government measurement of states and provinces and 49th on the state and local index. Its best showing, if it can be called that, came in takings and taxation, where it finished 46th in the all government rankings and 36th in state and local. From there, it's downhill: in size of government, the state was 50th at both all-government and subnational levels, and in labor market freedom 52nd (where Alberta and Nova Scotia beat it out) and 51st (Nova Scotia again), respectively. One bright spot: there is no general sales and use tax, and its effective state and local tax burden ranks 32nd among the 50 states at 10%.

Nebraska

Nebraska shows little disparity between its all-government and state and local overall rankings, coming in 20th and 21st, respectively. Size of government is the area where the state shows the most commitment to economic freedom, registering a score of 14th all-government and 4th state and local. Takings and taxation are 26th all-government and 31st state and local and

labor market freedom came in at 29th and 30th, respectively. Its effective state and local tax burden is 10.8%, ranking 13th among the states.

Nevada

Nevada shows one of the wider gaps in its all-national and state and local overall ratings, 3rd in the former and 11th in the latter. Its highest ratings are for labor market freedom, where a slight improvement in both measurements placed in 10th in all-government and 9th in state and local. The state's record on takings and taxation made it 15th in all-government and 17th state and local. Nevada also had a wide spread between its all-government ranking for size of government (where it placed 3rd) and the state and local ranking of 17th. Its effective state and local tax burden is low at 9.2%, placing it 43rd among the states. Nevada's general sales tax is among the highest in the country at 6.5% although, perhaps because of Las Vegas's influence, its beer tax, figured in dollars per gallon, is among the nation's lowest at 9¢.

New Hampshire

New Hampshire ranks 5th overall in the all-government measurement for 2000 and 6th in the state and local index. While the state ranked 38th in the all-government index in 1981, it has steadily improved since, and the 1st place finish this year and last is its highest ever. The state has risen from just over 80% of the national GDP in 1981 to 109%. New Hampshire has no general sales and use tax and its effective state and local sales tax burden is 48th among the 50 states. In the size of government rankings, New Hampshire holds the top spot in state and local and all-government rankings. For takings and discriminatory taxation, it's 2nd on both lists. Then, it slips on the economic banana peel: 29th in the all-government list for labor market freedom and 30th in state and local.

New Jersey

New Jersey came in at 20th for all government and 25th for state and local in the overall rankings, and has been consistent in its rankings in both indexes, ranging in the mid-20s for all-government and the 20s and 30s in the subnational index. Its best results were in the size of government rankings, where it was 5th in all government and 21st in state and local. For labor market freedom it held the 22nd spot in both measurements. It was least impressive when it came to takings and discriminatory taxation: 40th and 34th, respectively. Its general sales tax was at the high end at 6%, although at 10.5¢ its gasoline tax is among the country's lowest. New Jersey's effective state and local sales tax burden is the 23rd highest of the 50 states at 10.3%.

New Mexico

New Mexico's climate isn't particularly hospitable to economic freedom. It achieved its best overall ranking in the all-government index in 1981 (38th) and has fallen since. It now clocks in at 47th and 44th on the overall state and local comparison—tying an all-time low. New Mexico's highest marks come for all-government takings and taxes at 26th; for state and local it drops to 41st. From there it's downhill: 44th on both lists measuring labor market freedom; 39th in the state and local category for size of government, and 51st on the all-government index, tying Mississippi and trailing Alberta and British Columbia. Its effective state and local sales tax burden is 12th highest in the country at 10.9%. Driving and smoking is a bit less expensive than it is in most states because both those tax rates are on the low side.

New York

New York ranks 33rd overall in the all-government group, and its low-30s rankings the past three years are its best showing ever. The 39th ranking in state and local reflects its relatively lackluster performance in the three areas of measurement but still ties its best ranking there and is a far cry from the back-to-back 51st ratings in 1981 and 1985. In size of government, the state ranks 28th in the all-government index and 42nd in state and local. As for takings and taxation, the Empire State rates 32nd and 41st respectively. Its labor market freedom numbers placed it 29th in all-government and 30th state and local. The general sales and use tax is relatively low at 4% but the effective state and local tax burden is a killer—number 2 in the country at 12.3%.

North Carolina

North Carolina started slowly in the overall all-government index (25th in 1981), rallied to 6th by 1989, and has since settled into the mid-to-late teens. Labor

market freedom scores pull down North Carolina's overall rating to 15th in the current all-government section and 23rd in state and local. Its highest score is a 4th in the all-government list for takings and taxation, while it came in 17th in subnational. Size of government rankings placed it 12th in all-government and 14th in state and local but its placements in labor market freedom were 33rd and 36th, respectively. North Carolina's general sales and use tax at 4% was low for the states that have it, and its effective state and local tax burden was the 29th highest at 10.1%. Not surprisingly for a leading tobacco-growing state, its cigarette tax is the lowest at 5¢.

North Dakota

North Dakota shares with neighboring Montana dismal scores in all three areas of economic freedom, for an overall ranking of 48th in the all-government group and 47th in state and local. The state's only flirtation with the 30s is a 36th ranking state and local for takings and discriminatory taxation. Otherwise, it's 46th in all-government takings. In size of government, North Dakota is 46th in all-government and 48th state and local; for labor market freedom, 49th and 47th, respectively. The state's effective state and local sales tax burden is right in the middle of the pack, 26th at 10.2%. North Dakota's fall is somewhat perplexing; in 1981 it was 16th in the all-government index and 18th in the subnational. But the fall has been costly: the state's per-capita GDP has fallen 31 percentage points against the national average.

Ohio

Ohio registers overall at 29th on the all-government listings and slightly lower at 34th in the state and local list. That's typical: the state has wobbled through the 20s and 30s in the all-government index and the 30s and 40s in state and local since the measurements have been taken. Its overall rankings are an accurate reflection of its general position in the three major categories measuring economic freedom. The state is ranked 22nd in size of government in the all-government grouping but 37th in state and local, and 40th and 35th respectively in takings and taxation, and 26th and 27th in labor market freedom. Taxpayers will be saddened to know their effective state and local sales tax burden is the 9th highest among the 50 states at 11.2%.

Oklahoma

Oklahoma ranked 41st overall in all-government and 31st in state and local. The state has fallen considerably since 1981 when it was 5th in all-government and 10th in state and local—the worst decline among the 50 states. The size of government results found it at 44th in all-government and 21st in the state and local grouping, and 30th and 31st, respectively in the measurement for takings and taxation. The state showed a similarly close grouping in labor market freedom, 37th in both groups. Oklahoma's general sales tax was at the lower end of states that impose it at 4.5%, and only 5 states have a lower gasoline tax (Oklahoma's is 5¢). On the other hand, the state has the sixth-highest tax on spirits at $5.56 per gallon.

Oregon

Oregon has a substantial gap between its rating in the all-government measurement, where it ranks 29th, and in the state and local index where it comes in 42nd. But that's nothing compared to the disparity of its placements in the size of government category, 17th in all-government and 46th in state and local. This disparity is mainly due to a low ranking (53rd) in Area 1B at the subnational level, which was a result of high transfers—for example, welfare payments and subsidies to business—as a percentage of GDP. Government expenditures as a percentage of GDP are 31st highest in North America at the subnational level but only 18th at the all-government level. For takings and taxation, the state registers 20th all-government and 27th state and local, but takes a dive in labor market freedom, ranking 42nd and 44th respectively. Oregon doesn't impose a general sales tax, and its 9.4% effective state and local sales tax burden makes it only the 41st highest among the 50 states. Oregon has gradually improved its overall all-government rankings since the rating began, moving up from 44th in 1981.

Pennsylvania

Pennsylvania has been a predictable, steady state, with its overall all-government rankings in the low-to-mid 20s since 1989. This year, Pennsylvania ranks 20th in the all-government group and 14th in state and local in the overall ratings—an all-time high. Size of government isn't its strong suit, finishing 34th and 32nd, respectively. In takings and taxation, it's 26th in all-government, but comes up to 10th in the state and local

rankings. The state's best results are in labor market freedom, where it is 11th in both the lists. Its general sales and use tax is at the high end at 6% but its gasoline tax of 12¢ per gallon is among the lowest in the country, as is its tax on beer of 8¢. Pennsylvanians pay an effective state and local sales tax burden of 9.9%, only the 35th highest in the country.

Rhode Island

Rhode Island ranks 44th in the all-government list overall (and has never been higher than 41st, in 1989) and 46th on the state and local slate—and that's a step up from its 51st place finish from 1994 to 1996. Its size of government rankings are 34th in the all-government index and 48th state and local; and 33rd and 34th respectively in labor market freedom. And that's the good news. When it comes to takings and taxation, Rhode Island ranks 49th in the all-government measurement and 50th the subnational. It has the sixth-highest effective state and local sales tax burden at 11.3%, and its general sales tax of 7% is tied with Mississippi as the highest in the country.

South Carolina

South Carolina ranks 15th overall in the all-government category (down from single-digit ratings in 1985 and 1989) and 17th in the state and local measurements (also a drop from single digits in 1989 and 1993). It didn't earn the relatively high marks for its size of government ratings, 38th all-government and 28th state and local. Its rankings on takings and discriminatory taxation also left it in the middle of the pack, 23rd and 27th, respectively. On labor market freedom, however, the state was 4th in the all-government rankings, and 9th state and local. Drinkers probably pass through rather than pay its $1.08 per gallon beer and table wine taxes. The cigarette tax is the fourth-lowest in the country, and the 10% effective state and local sales tax burden ranks 30th among the states.

South Dakota

What a difference an adjective makes. Sitting due south of woeful North Dakota, South Dakota boasts a 9th place rating overall in the all-government measurements—and that represents a bit of backsliding from 4th place in 1997. It was 4th overall in the state and local index, again something of a retreat from its ranking from 1993 to 1997 when it was either 1st or 2nd. Its size of government is a middle 28th all-government but 4th state and local, and it finishes 12th and 7th, respectively in takings and taxation. South Dakota is strongest in labor market freedom, placing 8th and 3rd respectively. The state has a comparatively low general sales and use tax of 4%, and at 9.1% its effective state and local sales tax burden is only the 44th in the United States.

Tennessee

Tennessee has solid economic freedom credentials across the board and places 5th overall in the all-government category and 2nd in state and local—where it has been either 1st or 2nd since 1994. The only aberration is its ranking in the all-government list for size of government—28th. It's 4th in state and local. Otherwise, Tennessee ranks 4th in all-government and 3rd in state and local in takings and taxation, and 3rd in both groups for labor market freedom. Its general sales tax is on the high side at 6%, but the taxman has a hard fight in the state: effective state and local tax burden is the second lowest in the country at 8.4%. The tobacco tax is lower than most states at 13¢.

Texas

Texas is another state whose overall rankings are undone by a single category. It still manages to place 9th in the all-government ratings and 11th in state and local, though those rankings represent a drop in the all-government list (3rd in 1981, 1st in 1985) and subnational (1st in 1981, 2nd in 1985). The state's strong suit is takings and discriminatory taxation: 2nd all-government and 4th state and local (and Texas's effective state and local tax burden of 9% is 47th in the country —although its general sales tax is one of the country's highest at 6.25%). The state size of government ranking is 5th all-government and 8th state and local. The state stumbles when it comes to labor market freedom: 26th all-government and 27th state and local.

Utah

Utah ranks 29th in the all-government group overall— an improvement from the high 30s in the 1980s but a retreat from its 23rd ranking in 1999. It ranked 36th in the state and local index, again representing a drop off from the high 20s several years ago. Except for a 14th ranking in the all-government measurement for

size of government, Utah never threatens to join the elite states (its state and local ranking in the category is 34th). Utah placed 23rd all-government and 27th state and local in takings and taxation, and 42nd and 41st respectively for labor market freedom. Its general sales tax is lower than most states that impose it at 4.75%, but the effective state and local tax burden is the 8th highest in the country at 11.2%.

Vermont

Vermont is the opposite of some other states—a decent showing in one area helps to offset dismal ratings in the other two. The state's overall rankings were 35th in the all-government index and 39th in state and local—the latter showing considerable consistency since it operated in a narrow range of between 37th and 39th from 1993 to 2000. Its labor market freedom numbers are 17th all-government and 19th in the state and local measurement but after that it falls out of the top third in size of government: 34th all-government and 45th state and local. As for takings and taxation, it's at the bottom: 48th in both rankings. Vermont's effective state and local tax burden is the nation's tenth-highest at 11%.

Virginia

Virginia finished 35th overall in the 2000 all-government rankings, an example of a state that started badly in 1981 (48th), reached the high 20s, then fell back. It's subnational numbers have always been stronger; it ranked 18th in 1981, and was in single digits from 1985 to 1995. It now stands at 17th in the state and local index. Taxes are Virginia's strength: 8th in all-government and 7th state and local; the second-lowest general sales tax at 3.5%; and the tenth-lowest effective state and local tax burden at 9.4%. Smokers might as well not pay a tax: its cigarette tax of 2.5¢ is the lowest in the country. Other measures aren't as strong. Virginia scores 41st all-government and 10th state and local in the size of government category, and 37th and 34th respectively for labor market freedom.

Washington

Washington's overall rankings—35th all-government and 45th state and local—suggest there aren't many happy surprises, and there aren't, although its all-government ranking ties an all-time high, which suggests some improvement. The size of government ranking of 19th in the all-government measurement is respectable, but the state comes in at 47th state and local. Otherwise, Washington scores 37th in the all-government index and 41st state and local for labor market freedom and 43rd and 36th respectively for takings and discriminatory taxation. The general sales tax is on the high end at 6.5%, although its effective state and local tax burden is less onerous than some: 10.5%, making it 20th in the country.

West Virginia

West Virginia has the lowest per-capita GDP in the United States and the worst economic record through the 1990s. Its overall ranking in the all-government measurement is 50th. In state and local it's 52nd—making it the only state to finish lower than 50th in the category. Except for its labor market freedom rankings—37th all-government, 41st state and local—economic freedom is nowhere to be seen. West Virginia ranks 49th all-government and 52nd in takings and taxation, and for size of government can't even give Canada a run for its money, placing 56th and 55th respectively among the states and provinces.

Wisconsin

Wisconsin's mid-range showing in two categories is offset by a terrible record on taxation. Its overall rating is 26th all-government, up from its low of 35th in 1985, but slipping a bit from the last few years. It has moved in a relatively narrow range in the subnational index since 1989, and finished 28th. Size of government rankings are 19th for all-government and 30th state and local, and labor market freedom is also solid at 20th and 21st respectively. But, on taxation and discriminatory taxation, Wisconsinites are advised to hang onto their wallets: the state ranked 43rd for all-government and 36th state and local among the states and provinces. Its effective state and local tax burden is the third highest in the nation at 12%. At least it doesn't cost much for them to drown their sorrows: the tax on beer is among the country's lowest at 6.5¢.

Wyoming

Wyoming ranks 9th overall in the all-government measurement. Between 1981 and 1997, it never ranked lower than 4th, although the 2000 rankings was a bounce back from the 12th it received in 1999. It was 25th in the state and local index. Its strongest ratings are in labor market freedom: 11th in all-government and 13th in state and local. In takings and taxation it ranks 20th and 17th, respectively. Wyoming's one bad slip comes in the state and local list for size of government, where it rates only 42nd; its all-government ranking in the category is 19th. Wyoming is a relatively low-tax state—its effective state and local tax burden is 38th among the 50 states at 9.8%. Its general sales and use tax is low among the states that charge it at 4%. It beer tax of 2¢ is the lowest in the country, and its cigarette and gasoline taxes are among the lowest.

Appendix B: Detailed Tables

The following tables provide more information on economic freedom in the provinces and states at both the all-government and subnational levels. The first two tables provide a detailed summary of the scores for 2000. The remaining tables provide historical information both for the overall index and for each of Area 1. Size of Government; Area 2. Takings and Discriminatory Taxation; Area 3. Labor Market Freedom.

List of Tables

Appendix Table 1: Scores on All-Government Index (2000)

	Overall Index	Area 1	1A	1B	Area 2	2A	2B	2C	2D	Area 3	3A	3B	3C
Alberta	6.8	8.2	8.4	8.0	6.0	5.5	4.5	7.2	6.9	6.1	6.8	7.2	4.2
British Columbia	4.7	6.7	7.0	6.3	3.4	3.8	1.5	5.1	3.0	4.0	3.7	6.1	2.3
Manitoba	4.1	5.6	6.2	5.0	3.4	3.8	2.5	4.0	3.2	3.4	4.7	3.5	1.9
New Brunswick	4.4	4.8	4.7	4.8	3.9	4.6	2.5	5.2	3.2	4.4	4.3	4.3	4.6
Newfoundland	4.5	3.9	4.4	3.3	3.8	5.1	2.5	5.3	2.2	5.8	4.5	2.9	10.0
Nova Scotia	4.6	4.2	3.6	4.8	3.5	4.5	2.5	5.9	1.2	6.0	4.2	4.2	9.6
Ontario	5.5	7.6	8.0	7.1	4.0	4.4	3.5	4.5	3.6	4.9	5.1	7.0	2.7
Prince Edward Island	3.4	3.8	4.0	3.6	3.1	4.0	2.5	5.2	0.8	3.3	4.0	3.5	2.3
Quebec	4.1	6.1	6.6	5.5	2.9	3.4	2.5	2.6	3.2	3.4	4.1	5.3	0.8
Saskatchewan	4.4	5.9	6.6	5.2	3.7	4.4	2.5	4.4	3.6	3.7	5.2	3.5	2.3
Alabama	7.0	6.5	7.4	5.6	6.0	5.6	5.0	5.9	7.3	8.6	10.0	7.7	8.1
Alaska	6.1	5.5	4.1	6.9	6.2	2.5	6.0	6.7	9.4	6.6	6.7	6.2	6.9
Arizona	7.2	7.6	8.3	6.9	5.9	6.1	5.0	6.0	6.7	8.1	10.0	8.9	5.4
Arkansas	6.1	7.0	8.7	5.4	5.4	5.6	4.0	5.4	6.5	6.0	4.7	8.6	4.6
California	6.9	8.0	8.5	7.6	5.7	5.6	3.0	6.6	7.5	7.0	6.6	8.9	5.4
Colorado	7.7	8.3	8.4	8.2	6.3	6.1	5.0	6.7	7.5	8.4	6.5	9.0	9.6
Connecticut	7.2	8.1	8.9	7.4	5.5	5.1	5.0	4.4	7.6	8.1	7.1	9.4	7.7
Delaware	8.0	8.7	9.5	7.9	7.1	7.4	4.0	7.0	10.0	8.1	7.1	9.2	8.1
Florida	6.7	7.0	8.2	5.7	5.2	4.0	6.0	4.5	6.3	7.8	10.0	9.2	4.2
Georgia	7.3	8.3	8.9	7.7	6.3	6.7	4.0	7.3	7.1	7.4	7.6	8.7	5.8
Hawaii	6.4	6.9	6.4	7.3	5.4	6.2	3.0	6.4	6.0	6.8	6.1	7.5	6.9
Idaho	6.5	7.4	7.9	7.0	5.6	5.7	4.0	4.9	7.7	6.5	5.3	8.2	6.2
Illinois	7.1	8.4	9.3	7.4	6.0	5.8	5.0	4.9	8.3	7.1	6.4	9.1	5.8
Indiana	7.4	7.9	9.1	6.8	6.2	6.2	5.0	5.7	8.0	8.0	7.2	9.2	7.7
Iowa	6.4	7.6	8.6	6.6	5.4	5.4	4.0	4.7	7.7	6.3	5.6	8.6	4.6
Kansas	6.8	7.6	8.4	6.9	5.5	5.7	4.0	5.4	7.0	7.3	7.8	7.9	6.2
Kentucky	6.6	7.1	8.5	5.8	6.0	6.0	4.0	5.9	7.9	6.6	6.2	8.5	5.0
Louisiana	7.0	7.2	8.2	6.2	6.1	6.3	5.0	6.7	6.4	7.8	10.0	7.3	6.2
Maine	5.7	6.5	7.6	5.5	4.6	4.7	3.0	3.2	7.3	6.2	5.2	8.7	4.6
Maryland	6.3	6.9	6.5	7.4	5.8	4.8	5.0	4.8	8.5	6.1	6.2	7.4	4.6
Massachusetts	7.3	8.2	9.1	7.2	6.2	6.1	4.0	6.0	8.6	7.5	6.9	9.4	6.2
Michigan	6.9	7.7	8.8	6.6	5.5	4.7	5.0	5.0	7.4	7.6	5.9	8.9	8.1
Minnesota	6.9	8.3	9.0	7.5	5.5	4.9	4.0	5.1	7.8	7.1	6.4	9.2	5.8
Mississippi	6.3	5.9	7.0	4.8	5.3	5.4	5.0	4.8	6.1	7.8	10.0	7.2	6.2
Missouri	7.0	7.3	8.3	6.3	6.1	6.1	5.0	5.7	7.4	7.5	5.8	8.7	8.1
Montana	5.6	6.0	6.5	5.5	5.0	4.4	4.0	1.6	10.0	5.8	4.4	7.9	5.0
Nebraska	6.9	8.0	9.1	7.0	5.7	5.5	4.0	5.4	7.9	6.9	5.9	8.6	6.2
Nevada	7.5	8.6	9.3	7.9	6.0	6.1	6.0	5.2	6.9	7.9	6.4	10.0	7.3
New Hampshire	7.3	8.7	9.7	7.6	6.4	6.2	6.0	3.3	10.0	6.9	6.5	9.6	4.6
New Jersey	6.9	8.3	9.1	7.4	5.3	4.9	4.0	3.9	8.3	7.3	6.9	8.7	6.2
New Mexico	6.0	5.9	5.2	6.7	5.7	5.9	4.0	6.8	5.9	6.3	6.3	6.2	6.5
New York	6.6	7.5	8.7	6.3	5.5	4.8	4.0	5.4	7.7	6.9	7.4	8.1	5.4
North Carolina	7.0	8.1	9.0	7.1	6.3	6.4	4.0	6.8	8.1	6.7	6.2	8.5	5.4
North Dakota	5.8	6.5	7.0	5.9	5.0	5.1	4.0	3.3	7.5	6.0	5.3	8.2	4.6
Ohio	6.7	7.7	9.0	6.4	5.3	5.1	4.0	4.4	7.8	7.0	6.6	9.0	5.4
Oklahoma	6.3	6.8	7.8	5.9	5.6	5.6	4.0	5.7	7.0	6.5	4.9	8.0	6.5
Oregon	6.7	7.9	8.7	7.0	5.9	5.5	3.0	5.0	10.0	6.4	5.5	8.7	5.0
Pennsylvania	6.9	7.1	8.6	5.7	5.7	5.1	5.0	4.6	8.0	7.8	5.9	9.4	8.1
Rhode Island	6.2	7.1	8.2	5.9	4.8	4.7	3.0	3.3	8.0	6.7	6.1	9.0	5.0
South Carolina	7.0	7.0	7.9	6.2	5.8	5.8	4.0	5.7	7.5	8.1	10.0	7.8	6.5
South Dakota	7.2	7.5	8.2	6.7	6.1	6.1	6.0	5.3	7.1	8.0	5.6	8.8	9.6
Tennessee	7.3	7.5	8.8	6.1	6.3	6.3	6.0	6.6	6.4	8.2	10.0	9.1	5.4
Texas	7.2	8.3	8.9	7.6	6.4	6.5	6.0	5.6	7.4	7.0	7.5	8.5	5.0
Utah	6.7	8.0	8.0	8.0	5.8	5.9	4.0	6.4	6.8	6.4	5.6	8.1	5.4
Vermont	6.5	7.1	8.0	6.3	4.9	5.1	3.0	3.0	8.7	7.5	5.5	8.8	8.1
Virginia	6.5	6.9	6.0	7.9	6.2	6.2	4.0	5.9	8.6	6.5	6.4	7.7	5.4
Washington	6.5	7.8	8.4	7.2	5.2	4.8	6.0	4.5	5.5	6.5	6.6	8.2	4.6
West Virginia	5.6	5.4	7.6	3.3	4.8	4.7	4.0	2.8	7.5	6.5	4.7	7.0	7.7
Wisconsin	6.8	7.8	8.7	6.9	5.2	4.3	4.0	4.9	7.7	7.4	5.8	9.1	7.3
Wyoming	7.2	7.8	7.8	7.8	5.9	4.7	6.0	5.8	7.2	6.8	8.9	6.3	8.1

Appendix Table 2: Scores on Subnational Index (2000)

	Overall Index	Area 1	1A	1B	Area 2	2A	2B	2C	2D	Area 3	3A	3B	3C
Alberta	7.1	8.0	6.7	9.2	7.5	6.8	6.0	7.7	9.5	5.8	6.8	6.4	4.2
British Columbia	5.1	6.1	4.7	7.4	5.5	6.4	4.0	6.6	4.9	3.9	3.7	5.6	2.3
Manitoba	4.8	5.8	4.1	7.5	5.4	6.5	5.0	5.5	4.6	3.2	4.7	3.0	1.9
New Brunswick	5.2	5.3	2.7	7.9	6.1	7.2	5.0	7.0	5.0	4.3	4.3	4.1	4.6
Newfoundland	5.2	4.3	1.8	6.9	5.8	7.6	5.0	7.0	3.5	5.6	4.5	2.1	10.0
Nova Scotia	5.8	5.7	3.5	7.9	5.9	7.2	5.0	6.7	4.5	5.9	4.2	3.9	9.6
Ontario	6.0	7.3	6.6	7.9	5.8	7.4	5.0	5.6	5.1	5.0	5.1	7.2	2.7
Prince Edward Island	4.6	5.1	2.3	7.8	5.4	7.4	5.0	7.4	2.0	3.3	4.0	3.6	2.3
Quebec	4.4	5.3	4.5	6.1	4.6	5.8	4.0	4.1	4.6	3.2	4.1	4.8	0.8
Saskatchewan	5.0	6.0	4.0	8.0	5.4	6.3	5.0	5.4	5.0	3.4	5.2	2.8	2.3
Alabama	7.8	7.2	6.4	8.1	7.5	7.6	8.0	8.3	6.3	8.6	10.0	7.6	8.1
Alaska	6.1	4.2	1.8	6.7	7.2	2.9	10.0	6.8	9.2	6.8	6.7	6.9	6.9
Arizona	7.9	8.5	7.8	9.2	7.2	8.1	8.0	7.3	5.4	8.1	10.0	8.9	5.4
Arkansas	6.8	8.1	7.0	9.1	6.5	7.3	6.0	7.3	5.2	5.9	4.7	8.3	4.6
California	6.9	7.4	7.3	7.4	6.4	7.5	4.0	7.8	6.5	6.9	6.6	8.7	5.4
Colorado	8.2	8.9	8.1	9.7	7.4	8.2	7.0	8.0	6.6	8.4	6.5	9.1	9.6
Connecticut	7.7	8.1	7.8	8.4	7.1	8.5	7.5	5.6	6.7	8.0	7.1	9.2	7.7
Delaware	8.4	8.8	8.1	9.6	8.3	8.6	7.5	7.2	10.0	8.0	7.1	8.9	8.1
Florida	7.6	8.2	6.8	9.5	7.0	7.2	10.0	5.9	4.9	7.8	10.0	9.1	4.2
Georgia	7.9	9.0	8.3	9.7	7.2	8.3	6.0	8.6	6.0	7.4	7.6	8.8	5.8
Hawaii	6.9	7.2	6.5	8.0	6.2	7.6	5.0	7.8	4.5	7.1	6.1	8.4	6.9
Idaho	6.7	7.4	6.6	8.1	6.3	7.4	5.0	6.2	6.8	6.5	5.3	7.9	6.2
Illinois	7.6	8.4	8.0	8.8	7.4	8.3	8.0	5.8	7.6	7.0	6.4	8.9	5.8
Indiana	8.1	8.7	7.6	9.9	7.7	8.3	8.0	7.2	7.2	8.0	7.2	8.9	7.7
Iowa	7.0	7.8	6.6	9.1	6.9	7.4	7.5	6.1	6.8	6.1	5.6	8.2	4.6
Kansas	7.5	8.4	7.2	9.7	6.8	8.1	6.0	7.4	5.9	7.2	7.8	7.5	6.2
Kentucky	7.2	8.0	7.6	8.4	7.0	7.6	6.0	7.4	7.1	6.5	6.2	8.3	5.0
Louisiana	7.7	8.0	6.7	9.3	7.3	7.7	8.5	7.9	5.1	7.6	10.0	6.8	6.2
Maine	6.3	7.1	6.1	8.2	5.5	6.7	5.0	4.1	6.3	6.2	5.2	8.6	4.6
Maryland	7.3	8.0	7.6	8.3	7.5	7.9	7.0	6.9	8.0	6.5	6.2	8.9	4.6
Massachusetts	7.9	8.5	8.3	8.8	7.7	8.6	7.0	7.2	8.1	7.5	6.9	9.4	6.2
Michigan	7.4	7.7	6.6	8.7	7.0	7.0	8.0	6.7	6.4	7.5	5.9	8.5	8.1
Minnesota	7.1	7.9	7.3	8.4	6.4	6.9	5.5	6.3	6.9	7.0	6.4	8.9	5.8
Mississippi	7.2	7.5	5.6	9.5	6.3	7.0	7.0	6.7	4.7	7.6	10.0	6.8	6.2
Missouri	7.9	8.5	7.8	9.3	7.6	8.2	8.0	7.7	6.4	7.5	5.8	8.6	8.1
Montana	6.2	6.3	4.8	7.9	6.5	6.8	6.5	2.9	10.0	5.8	4.4	8.1	5.0
Nebraska	7.5	8.8	7.8	9.9	6.8	7.3	6.0	6.9	7.0	6.8	5.9	8.3	6.2
Nevada	7.8	8.3	8.1	8.5	7.2	8.0	10.0	5.2	5.7	7.9	6.4	10.0	7.3
New Hampshire	8.0	9.1	8.6	9.6	8.1	8.9	10.0	3.6	10.0	6.8	6.5	9.3	4.6
New Jersey	7.3	8.0	7.6	8.3	6.7	7.9	6.5	4.8	7.7	7.2	6.9	8.5	6.2
New Mexico	6.6	7.2	5.6	8.8	6.4	7.1	5.5	8.5	4.4	6.3	6.3	6.2	6.5
New York	6.8	7.1	6.6	7.7	6.4	6.7	6.0	6.2	6.9	6.8	7.4	7.7	5.4
North Carolina	7.4	8.4	7.8	9.1	7.2	7.8	5.5	8.0	7.4	6.6	6.2	8.1	5.4
North Dakota	6.3	6.4	5.4	7.4	6.5	7.1	8.0	4.2	6.5	6.1	5.3	8.3	4.6
Ohio	7.0	7.3	7.6	7.1	6.6	7.0	7.0	5.5	7.0	6.9	6.6	8.8	5.4
Oklahoma	7.1	8.0	6.8	9.2	6.8	7.5	6.0	7.8	5.8	6.5	4.9	8.0	6.5
Oregon	6.7	6.9	6.8	7.1	6.9	7.4	4.0	6.2	10.0	6.3	5.5	8.5	5.0
Pennsylvania	7.7	7.6	7.1	8.2	7.5	7.6	9.0	6.2	7.2	7.8	5.9	9.5	8.1
Rhode Island	6.4	6.4	6.8	6.0	6.0	7.0	5.0	4.6	7.3	6.7	6.1	9.1	5.0
South Carolina	7.6	7.8	6.7	8.9	6.9	7.6	6.0	7.4	6.5	7.9	10.0	7.3	6.5
South Dakota	8.1	8.8	7.6	10.0	7.6	7.9	10.0	6.4	6.0	8.1	5.6	9.0	9.6
Tennessee	8.3	8.8	8.2	9.4	7.8	8.1	10.0	8.2	5.0	8.1	10.0	9.0	5.4
Texas	7.8	8.7	8.2	9.2	7.7	8.2	10.0	6.1	6.4	6.9	7.5	8.2	5.0
Utah	6.9	7.4	6.9	7.9	6.9	7.2	7.0	7.6	5.7	6.4	5.6	8.3	5.4
Vermont	6.8	7.0	6.2	7.8	6.1	7.4	5.0	3.7	8.2	7.4	5.5	8.7	8.1
Virginia	7.6	8.6	7.8	9.3	7.6	8.2	7.0	7.2	8.0	6.7	6.4	8.5	5.4
Washington	6.5	6.5	7.5	5.4	6.5	7.0	10.0	5.3	3.8	6.4	6.6	8.1	4.6
West Virginia	5.8	5.3	5.6	4.9	5.8	6.6	6.5	3.7	6.6	6.4	4.7	6.9	7.7
Wisconsin	7.2	7.7	6.6	8.8	6.5	6.2	7.0	5.9	6.8	7.3	5.8	8.7	7.3
Wyoming	7.3	7.1	5.9	8.2	7.2	6.4	10.0	6.3	6.2	7.6	8.9	5.9	8.1

Appendix Table 3: Overall Scores on All-Government Index

	1981	1985	1989	1993	1994	1995	1996	1997	1998	1999	2000	Rank*
Alberta	6.0	5.9	5.8	5.7	6.1	6.2	6.4	6.6	6.4	6.6	6.8	26
British Columbia	5.1	5.0	5.4	4.5	4.5	4.4	4.4	4.5	4.5	4.6	4.7	53
Manitoba	4.5	4.1	4.2	3.5	3.6	3.7	4.0	4.1	4.2	4.0	4.1	58
New Brunswick	2.1	3.4	4.0	3.4	3.5	3.8	3.8	3.9	4.1	4.3	4.4	56
Newfoundland	3.4	3.1	3.7	2.7	3.0	3.3	3.2	3.4	3.7	4.3	4.5	55
Nova Scotia	1.8	3.1	4.1	3.6	3.6	3.9	4.0	4.2	4.3	4.5	4.6	54
Ontario	5.4	5.5	5.6	4.6	4.6	4.8	4.9	5.0	5.2	5.3	5.5	52
Prince Edward Island	3.7	3.2	3.5	2.8	2.9	3.0	3.1	2.9	3.2	3.3	3.4	60
Quebec	3.4	3.6	4.1	3.3	3.5	3.5	3.6	3.7	3.8	3.9	4.1	58
Saskatchewan	4.5	4.1	4.0	3.6	3.9	4.2	4.4	4.5	4.3	4.3	4.4	56
Alabama	6.5	6.8	7.5	7.1	7.0	7.1	7.0	7.0	7.1	7.0	7.0	15
Alaska	7.4	7.3	7.2	6.1	6.2	6.3	6.3	6.3	5.9	6.1	6.1	45
Arizona	6.2	6.5	6.9	6.7	6.8	6.9	7.0	7.1	7.2	7.1	7.2	9
Arkansas	5.8	5.8	6.7	6.3	6.3	6.3	6.3	6.3	6.1	6.1	6.1	45
California	6.0	6.4	7.2	6.5	6.5	6.5	6.6	6.7	6.7	6.8	6.9	20
Colorado	6.9	6.8	7.3	7.4	7.3	7.4	7.5	7.5	7.6	7.6	7.7	2
Connecticut	5.9	6.8	7.5	7.2	7.1	7.1	7.1	7.2	7.2	7.2	7.2	9
Delaware	6.9	7.2	8.1	7.8	7.7	7.8	7.8	8.0	7.9	8.0	8.0	1
Florida	6.4	6.8	7.3	6.7	6.6	6.5	6.6	6.6	6.6	6.7	6.7	29
Georgia	6.4	6.6	7.4	7.0	7.0	7.1	7.1	7.2	7.3	7.3	7.3	5
Hawaii	5.8	6.2	7.2	6.7	6.4	6.4	6.2	6.3	6.3	6.3	6.4	39
Idaho	6.0	6.0	6.5	6.4	6.4	6.5	6.4	6.4	6.3	6.4	6.5	35
Illinois	6.5	6.7	7.4	7.1	7.1	7.0	7.1	7.1	7.1	7.1	7.1	14
Indiana	6.6	6.8	7.5	7.3	7.3	7.3	7.3	7.3	7.4	7.4	7.4	4
Iowa	7.0	6.7	6.7	6.3	6.5	6.4	6.6	6.7	6.5	6.4	6.4	39
Kansas	6.4	6.4	6.9	6.6	6.5	6.5	6.7	6.8	6.8	6.8	6.8	26
Kentucky	6.2	6.3	6.9	6.6	6.5	6.5	6.5	6.5	6.5	6.6	6.6	33
Louisiana	8.0	7.5	7.8	7.0	7.0	7.1	7.1	7.2	7.0	7.0	7.0	15
Maine	5.1	5.6	6.4	5.7	5.6	5.8	5.7	5.6	5.5	5.7	5.7	49
Maryland	4.8	5.6	6.7	6.0	6.0	6.0	6.1	6.1	6.1	6.2	6.3	41
Massachusetts	5.6	6.6	7.3	7.0	6.9	6.9	6.9	7.0	7.1	7.2	7.3	5
Michigan	5.9	6.5	7.2	6.9	7.0	7.0	7.0	7.0	6.9	6.9	6.9	20
Minnesota	6.2	6.3	6.9	6.6	6.6	6.5	6.7	6.8	6.8	6.9	6.9	20
Mississippi	6.4	6.4	6.9	6.7	6.6	6.6	6.4	6.4	6.4	6.4	6.3	41
Missouri	7.0	7.2	7.3	7.0	7.0	7.0	6.9	7.0	7.0	7.0	7.0	15
Montana	6.3	5.6	6.0	5.8	5.7	5.5	5.6	5.6	5.6	5.6	5.6	50
Nebraska	6.5	6.5	7.0	6.7	6.7	6.7	6.8	6.8	6.8	6.8	6.9	20
Nevada	6.5	6.8	7.9	7.4	7.5	7.4	7.5	7.5	7.4	7.5	7.5	3
New Hampshire	5.8	6.9	7.4	6.7	6.8	6.9	7.1	7.1	7.2	7.3	7.3	5
New Jersey	5.9	6.6	7.3	6.7	6.6	6.6	6.7	6.8	6.8	6.9	6.9	20
New Mexico	5.8	5.6	5.7	6.1	6.1	5.9	5.9	6.1	5.9	5.9	6.0	47
New York	5.7	6.1	6.8	6.3	6.2	6.2	6.3	6.4	6.6	6.6	6.6	33
North Carolina	6.2	6.7	7.5	7.0	6.9	6.9	6.9	7.0	6.9	7.0	7.0	15
North Dakota	6.4	5.8	5.8	5.9	5.9	5.9	6.1	5.8	5.9	5.8	5.8	48
Ohio	6.3	6.4	6.9	6.5	6.5	6.5	6.5	6.7	6.8	6.7	6.7	29
Oklahoma	7.0	6.6	6.7	6.4	6.1	6.1	6.3	6.3	6.2	6.2	6.3	41
Oregon	5.7	5.9	6.5	6.5	6.4	6.5	6.7	6.7	6.7	6.7	6.7	29
Pennsylvania	6.1	6.4	7.2	6.9	6.7	6.8	6.8	6.7	6.8	6.8	6.9	20
Rhode Island	5.2	5.7	6.6	5.9	5.7	5.7	5.8	6.0	6.1	6.0	6.2	44
South Carolina	6.6	6.8	7.5	7.0	6.9	7.0	7.0	7.0	7.0	7.0	7.0	15
South Dakota	6.3	6.7	7.3	7.3	7.2	7.2	7.3	7.3	7.1	7.2	7.2	9
Tennessee	6.4	6.9	7.7	7.2	7.3	7.3	7.2	7.3	7.3	7.3	7.3	5
Texas	7.6	7.5	7.4	7.1	7.0	7.0	7.1	7.2	7.2	7.2	7.2	9
Utah	5.8	6.0	6.4	6.4	6.5	6.6	6.9	6.7	6.7	6.8	6.7	29
Vermont	6.0	6.3	7.3	6.7	6.6	6.4	6.4	6.5	6.5	6.5	6.5	35
Virginia	5.5	6.2	7.1	6.6	6.4	6.3	6.5	6.4	6.5	6.5	6.5	35
Washington	5.7	5.9	6.6	6.3	6.2	5.9	6.1	6.2	6.3	6.5	6.5	35
West Virginia	5.8	5.4	6.3	5.6	5.7	5.7	5.7	5.6	5.5	5.5	5.6	50
Wisconsin	6.2	6.2	7.0	6.7	6.7	6.8	6.7	6.8	6.8	6.8	6.8	26
Wyoming	8.0	7.3	7.8	7.5	7.4	7.3	7.4	7.3	7.2	7.1	7.2	9

* Rank out of 60 for year 2000.

Appendix Table 4: Overall Scores on Subnational Index

	1981	1985	1989	1993	1994	1995	1996	1997	1998	1999	2000	Rank*
Alberta	6.5	6.0	5.8	5.7	6.3	6.5	6.8	7.0	7.0	7.1	7.1	31
British Columbia	5.2	5.1	5.7	4.7	4.7	4.6	4.7	4.8	5.0	5.1	5.1	56
Manitoba	5.4	4.8	4.5	3.8	4.1	4.2	4.6	4.6	4.9	4.7	4.8	58
New Brunswick	4.1	4.2	4.6	4.1	4.3	4.5	4.5	4.6	4.9	5.2	5.2	54
Newfoundland	3.8	3.8	4.1	3.3	3.5	3.7	3.7	4.0	4.6	5.0	5.2	54
Nova Scotia	3.8	4.6	5.1	4.7	4.8	5.0	5.3	5.3	5.6	5.8	5.8	52
Ontario	6.2	6.1	5.9	4.5	4.8	4.8	5.2	5.5	5.7	6.0	6.0	51
Prince Edward Island	4.4	4.3	4.2	3.6	3.7	4.0	4.1	4.0	4.4	4.5	4.6	59
Quebec	3.4	3.4	4.1	2.9	3.3	3.2	3.6	3.8	4.1	4.3	4.4	60
Saskatchewan	4.7	4.4	4.3	3.7	4.3	4.5	4.7	4.9	4.8	4.8	5.0	57
Alabama	7.9	8.0	8.1	7.8	7.9	7.9	7.9	7.9	7.8	7.8	7.8	11
Alaska	8.0	7.4	6.8	5.9	6.0	5.9	6.1	6.1	5.8	6.1	6.1	50
Arizona	7.7	7.6	7.1	7.0	7.2	7.3	7.6	7.7	7.9	7.9	7.9	7
Arkansas	6.8	6.8	7.1	6.8	6.9	6.9	6.9	6.9	6.8	6.8	6.8	39
California	6.4	6.6	6.8	6.0	6.1	6.2	6.3	6.5	6.7	6.9	6.9	36
Colorado	8.1	7.6	7.5	7.6	7.7	7.7	7.8	7.9	8.2	8.2	8.2	3
Connecticut	7.4	7.8	7.9	7.1	7.2	7.2	7.4	7.5	7.6	7.7	7.7	14
Delaware	6.9	7.7	8.1	7.9	8.0	8.0	8.0	8.1	8.2	8.2	8.4	1
Florida	8.3	8.2	7.8	7.2	7.4	7.3	7.4	7.5	7.6	7.6	7.6	17
Georgia	7.6	7.5	7.5	7.4	7.5	7.5	7.5	7.7	7.8	7.9	7.9	7
Hawaii	6.5	7.0	7.5	6.7	6.5	6.3	6.3	6.5	6.7	6.8	6.9	36
Idaho	6.8	6.7	6.7	6.6	6.7	6.5	6.4	6.6	6.5	6.7	6.7	42
Illinois	6.9	7.3	7.6	7.2	7.4	7.3	7.4	7.5	7.6	7.6	7.6	17
Indiana	7.5	7.8	7.8	7.9	7.9	7.9	8.0	8.0	8.1	8.1	8.1	4
Iowa	7.7	7.2	6.7	6.4	6.7	6.6	6.9	7.0	7.0	7.0	7.0	34
Kansas	7.1	7.2	7.2	6.8	6.8	6.8	7.0	7.2	7.4	7.5	7.5	21
Kentucky	7.0	7.3	7.2	7.0	7.1	7.0	7.0	7.1	7.2	7.2	7.2	28
Louisiana	8.7	7.9	7.9	7.6	7.7	7.8	7.8	7.8	7.7	7.6	7.7	14
Maine	5.8	6.2	6.6	5.8	6.0	6.0	6.1	5.9	6.0	6.3	6.3	47
Maryland	6.5	7.1	7.3	6.8	6.9	6.9	7.0	7.0	7.1	7.3	7.3	25
Massachusetts	6.6	7.6	7.5	7.1	7.3	7.2	7.4	7.5	7.8	7.9	7.9	7
Michigan	5.7	6.7	6.8	6.7	7.1	7.1	7.3	7.3	7.3	7.4	7.4	23
Minnesota	6.1	6.5	6.5	6.3	6.5	6.5	6.7	6.9	6.9	7.1	7.1	31
Mississippi	7.6	7.4	7.3	7.3	7.4	7.3	7.2	7.1	7.2	7.2	7.2	28
Missouri	8.3	8.5	7.9	7.8	7.9	7.8	7.9	7.9	7.9	7.9	7.9	7
Montana	7.0	6.0	5.7	5.8	5.8	5.6	5.7	6.0	6.1	6.2	6.2	49
Nebraska	7.2	7.1	7.2	7.1	7.2	7.2	7.3	7.3	7.3	7.5	7.5	21
Nevada	7.3	7.4	7.5	7.0	7.4	7.4	7.6	7.6	7.8	7.8	7.8	11
New Hampshire	7.3	8.0	7.9	6.7	7.3	7.5	7.7	7.8	7.9	8.0	8.0	6
New Jersey	6.5	7.2	7.4	6.6	6.7	6.6	6.7	7.0	7.1	7.3	7.3	25
New Mexico	7.2	6.8	6.4	6.7	6.7	6.5	6.6	6.7	6.6	6.6	6.6	44
New York	5.5	5.9	6.4	5.7	5.9	5.8	6.2	6.4	6.7	6.8	6.8	39
North Carolina	7.0	7.4	7.5	7.1	7.2	7.2	7.2	7.3	7.3	7.4	7.4	23
North Dakota	7.4	6.3	5.6	5.8	6.2	6.4	6.5	6.2	6.3	6.3	6.3	47
Ohio	6.6	6.6	6.8	6.1	6.4	6.4	6.5	6.8	7.0	6.9	7.0	34
Oklahoma	7.8	7.4	7.0	6.8	6.6	6.6	6.9	7.0	7.0	7.0	7.1	31
Oregon	5.9	6.0	6.3	6.2	6.6	6.6	6.6	6.6	6.9	6.9	6.7	42
Pennsylvania	6.6	7.1	7.5	7.0	7.2	7.2	7.3	7.3	7.6	7.6	7.7	14
Rhode Island	5.5	6.1	6.6	5.4	5.4	5.3	5.6	5.9	6.3	6.3	6.4	46
South Carolina	7.6	7.7	7.8	7.4	7.4	7.4	7.4	7.5	7.6	7.6	7.6	17
South Dakota	7.5	7.7	7.7	8.0	8.0	8.0	8.2	8.2	8.0	8.1	8.1	4
Tennessee	8.0	8.2	8.2	7.7	8.1	8.1	8.1	8.1	8.3	8.3	8.3	2
Texas	8.9	8.4	7.6	7.4	7.5	7.5	7.6	7.7	7.8	7.8	7.8	11
Utah	7.0	6.8	6.5	6.6	6.8	6.9	7.1	7.0	7.1	6.9	6.9	36
Vermont	5.9	6.4	7.2	6.4	6.5	6.4	6.5	6.6	6.7	6.8	6.8	39
Virginia	7.4	7.8	7.9	7.4	7.5	7.5	7.5	7.5	7.6	7.6	7.6	17
Washington	6.6	6.3	6.4	5.9	6.0	5.5	5.8	6.1	6.4	6.5	6.5	45
West Virginia	5.6	5.2	6.0	5.0	5.5	5.8	5.7	5.6	5.8	5.8	5.8	52
Wisconsin	6.5	6.3	6.8	6.7	6.8	6.8	6.8	6.9	7.1	7.1	7.2	28
Wyoming	8.5	7.3	7.2	7.2	7.2	7.3	7.3	7.4	7.3	7.3	7.3	25

* Rank out of 60 for year 2000.

Appendix Table 5: Scores for Area 1 on All-Government Index

	1981	1985	1989	1993	1994	1995	1996	1997	1998	1999	2000	Rank*
Alberta	8.7	7.5	7.1	7.1	7.7	7.9	8.1	8.3	8.1	8.2	8.2	10
British Columbia	7.3	6.5	6.9	6.3	6.5	6.6	6.6	6.7	6.6	6.7	6.7	45
Manitoba	6.5	5.6	5.5	4.6	5.0	5.2	5.5	5.7	5.7	5.6	5.6	54
New Brunswick	1.8	3.8	4.4	3.6	3.8	4.4	4.5	4.5	4.6	4.8	4.8	57
Newfoundland	3.6	2.7	2.9	1.5	1.9	2.6	2.6	2.7	3.1	3.9	3.9	59
Nova Scotia	0.8	2.8	3.7	2.8	3.0	3.3	3.6	3.8	4.0	4.2	4.2	58
Ontario	7.5	7.3	7.6	6.2	6.6	6.8	7.1	7.3	7.4	7.6	7.6	24
Prince Edward Island	3.0	1.8	2.7	2.4	2.8	3.2	3.6	3.3	3.7	3.8	3.8	60
Quebec	5.4	5.3	6.0	4.8	5.1	5.4	5.6	5.9	5.9	6.1	6.1	49
Saskatchewan	6.8	4.8	4.9	4.9	5.4	5.8	6.3	6.3	6.0	5.9	5.9	51
Alabama	6.6	6.7	6.9	6.3	6.3	6.5	6.4	6.5	6.6	6.5	6.5	46
Alaska	9.0	8.2	6.9	5.6	5.7	6.3	6.3	6.3	5.6	5.6	5.5	55
Arizona	6.6	6.9	6.8	6.7	7.1	7.1	7.3	7.5	7.6	7.5	7.6	24
Arkansas	6.9	6.8	7.2	6.9	7.1	7.1	7.1	7.0	7.0	7.1	7.0	38
California	6.9	7.4	7.9	7.2	7.3	7.4	7.5	7.7	7.8	8.0	8.0	14
Colorado	7.6	7.6	7.3	7.4	7.5	7.6	7.7	8.1	8.2	8.3	8.3	5
Connecticut	6.9	7.5	7.8	7.7	7.8	7.7	7.8	8.0	8.1	8.1	8.1	12
Delaware	7.9	8.3	8.6	8.5	8.5	8.6	8.6	8.8	8.7	8.7	8.7	1
Florida	6.8	7.1	7.2	6.5	6.5	6.5	6.6	6.7	6.9	6.9	7.0	38
Georgia	7.2	7.8	8.1	7.6	7.7	7.8	7.9	8.1	8.2	8.3	8.3	5
Hawaii	6.7	7.1	7.7	7.3	7.1	7.0	6.9	7.0	6.9	6.9	6.9	41
Idaho	7.2	7.0	7.1	7.1	7.3	7.3	7.2	7.2	7.2	7.4	7.4	31
Illinois	8.1	8.2	8.4	8.1	8.2	8.2	8.2	8.3	8.3	8.4	8.4	4
Indiana	7.7	7.6	8.0	7.6	7.7	7.8	7.8	7.9	8.0	8.0	7.9	17
Iowa	8.1	7.5	7.7	7.3	7.6	7.5	7.7	7.8	7.6	7.6	7.6	24
Kansas	7.3	7.2	7.4	7.2	7.2	7.2	7.4	7.6	7.6	7.7	7.6	24
Kentucky	6.8	6.8	7.3	7.0	7.2	6.9	7.0	7.0	6.9	7.2	7.1	34
Louisiana	9.0	8.3	7.6	6.6	6.6	7.0	7.1	7.2	7.1	7.1	7.2	33
Maine	6.3	6.8	7.0	5.9	6.1	6.4	6.2	6.2	6.2	6.5	6.5	46
Maryland	5.6	6.5	7.4	6.6	6.6	6.6	6.7	6.8	6.8	6.9	6.9	41
Massachusetts	6.2	7.2	7.5	7.3	7.4	7.5	7.6	7.7	8.0	8.1	8.2	10
Michigan	7.2	7.6	7.7	7.2	7.6	7.5	7.5	7.5	7.6	7.7	7.7	22
Minnesota	7.5	7.6	7.9	7.5	7.7	7.7	7.9	8.1	8.2	8.2	8.3	5
Mississippi	6.2	6.2	6.1	5.9	6.0	6.0	5.8	6.0	6.1	6.0	5.9	51
Missouri	6.6	6.9	7.1	6.9	7.0	7.1	6.8	7.3	7.3	7.3	7.3	32
Montana	7.8	6.8	6.5	6.3	6.3	6.0	6.0	6.1	6.1	6.1	6.0	50
Nebraska	7.9	7.7	7.8	7.7	7.8	7.9	7.9	7.9	8.0	8.0	8.0	14
Nevada	7.4	7.4	8.2	7.9	8.2	8.3	8.3	8.5	8.5	8.6	8.6	3
New Hampshire	7.2	8.1	8.3	7.8	7.8	7.9	8.1	8.3	8.4	8.6	8.7	1
New Jersey	7.5	7.9	8.3	7.8	7.8	7.8	8.0	8.0	8.1	8.2	8.3	5
New Mexico	6.3	5.9	5.3	5.6	6.3	5.9	6.0	6.3	6.0	5.9	5.9	51
New York	7.1	7.4	7.6	7.0	7.0	6.9	7.1	7.2	7.4	7.4	7.5	28
North Carolina	7.7	8.1	8.3	7.7	7.8	7.8	7.7	7.8	8.0	8.0	8.1	12
North Dakota	8.0	7.0	6.2	6.1	6.5	6.5	6.8	6.5	6.7	6.5	6.5	46
Ohio	7.5	7.4	7.6	7.3	7.5	7.5	7.5	7.6	7.8	7.8	7.7	22
Oklahoma	8.4	7.9	7.3	6.8	6.7	6.6	6.8	6.9	6.9	6.8	6.8	44
Oregon	7.2	7.1	7.4	7.1	7.3	7.3	7.6	7.7	7.7	7.8	7.9	17
Pennsylvania	7.1	7.0	7.4	6.9	7.0	7.0	7.0	7.1	7.2	7.1	7.1	34
Rhode Island	6.2	6.8	7.2	6.2	6.3	6.3	6.4	6.7	6.9	6.8	7.1	34
South Carolina	6.7	7.0	7.3	6.8	6.7	6.9	6.9	7.0	7.1	7.0	7.0	38
South Dakota	7.2	7.1	7.3	7.4	7.5	7.5	7.6	7.6	7.6	7.5	7.5	28
Tennessee	6.8	7.2	7.6	7.3	7.4	7.4	7.3	7.4	7.4	7.5	7.5	28
Texas	8.9	8.5	8.2	7.9	7.9	7.9	7.9	8.2	8.2	8.2	8.3	5
Utah	6.9	7.0	6.9	7.2	7.5	7.4	7.8	7.9	8.0	8.0	8.0	14
Vermont	7.0	7.2	7.7	7.2	7.3	7.0	7.0	7.2	7.2	7.1	7.1	34
Virginia	5.9	6.8	7.3	6.7	6.8	6.5	6.8	6.9	6.9	6.9	6.9	41
Washington	6.8	6.8	7.4	7.3	7.3	7.1	7.2	7.4	7.6	7.8	7.8	19
West Virginia	6.9	6.3	6.2	5.2	5.6	5.5	5.5	5.4	5.4	5.5	5.4	56
Wisconsin	7.4	7.3	7.7	7.5	7.6	7.6	7.7	7.7	7.9	7.8	7.8	19
Wyoming	9.7	8.7	8.1	7.9	7.8	7.8	7.9	7.9	7.8	7.7	7.8	19

* Rank out of 60 for year 2000.

Appendix Table 6: Scores for Area 1 on Subnational Index

	1981	1985	1989	1993	1994	1995	1996	1997	1998	1999	2000	Rank*
Alberta	7.5	6.2	6.0	5.7	6.9	7.2	7.6	7.8	7.9	8.0	8.0	21
British Columbia	5.9	5.8	6.6	5.1	5.3	5.3	5.4	5.5	6.0	6.1	6.1	51
Manitoba	6.6	5.8	5.5	3.8	4.6	4.8	5.4	5.6	6.1	5.8	5.8	53
New Brunswick	4.3	4.6	5.1	4.0	4.2	4.6	4.8	4.7	5.2	5.3	5.3	55
Newfoundland	3.3	3.4	3.3	1.6	1.9	2.3	2.4	2.8	3.9	4.4	4.3	59
Nova Scotia	3.5	5.0	5.5	4.4	4.7	4.6	5.2	5.0	5.5	5.7	5.7	54
Ontario	7.2	7.2	7.2	4.6	5.3	5.5	6.1	6.6	7.1	7.3	7.3	37
Prince Edward Island	3.7	4.1	4.0	2.9	3.6	4.1	4.5	4.6	5.1	5.1	5.1	58
Quebec	3.9	3.7	5.1	2.5	3.2	3.3	3.9	4.4	5.2	5.3	5.3	55
Saskatchewan	4.8	4.3	4.6	4.0	5.2	5.3	5.9	6.3	6.1	6.0	6.0	52
Alabama	7.5	7.8	8.1	7.6	7.6	7.6	7.6	7.7	7.3	7.2	7.2	39
Alaska	8.5	7.0	5.8	4.0	3.9	4.2	4.5	4.7	4.3	4.2	4.2	60
Arizona	8.1	8.2	7.3	7.1	7.5	7.6	7.9	8.1	8.5	8.5	8.5	11
Arkansas	7.8	8.0	8.2	7.6	8.0	7.7	7.7	7.8	8.0	8.1	8.1	19
California	6.6	6.9	7.1	5.1	5.6	5.6	6.1	6.6	7.1	7.4	7.4	34
Colorado	8.1	7.8	7.6	7.5	7.7	7.5	7.7	8.2	9.0	8.9	8.9	3
Connecticut	7.7	8.4	8.3	6.5	6.7	6.7	7.4	7.7	8.0	8.1	8.1	19
Delaware	6.9	8.3	8.6	8.2	8.3	8.2	8.2	8.5	8.8	8.8	8.8	4
Florida	8.8	8.8	8.3	7.2	7.8	7.5	7.6	7.8	8.2	8.2	8.2	18
Georgia	8.4	8.8	8.6	8.2	8.5	8.4	8.3	8.6	8.9	9.0	9.0	2
Hawaii	7.1	7.8	8.6	6.9	6.7	6.1	6.4	6.7	7.2	7.2	7.2	39
Idaho	7.6	7.4	7.9	7.3	7.4	6.8	6.7	7.1	7.3	7.4	7.4	34
Illinois	6.4	7.6	8.2	7.6	7.9	7.7	7.9	8.1	8.4	8.4	8.4	14
Indiana	7.6	8.4	8.7	8.3	8.5	8.3	8.4	8.6	8.8	8.7	8.7	8
Iowa	7.5	7.2	7.7	7.1	7.6	7.3	7.7	7.9	7.9	7.8	7.8	28
Kansas	7.8	8.1	7.8	7.2	7.4	7.4	7.7	8.1	8.4	8.4	8.4	14
Kentucky	6.9	8.0	8.2	7.7	7.8	7.7	7.7	7.9	8.1	8.0	8.0	21
Louisiana	9.1	8.1	8.2	7.6	8.0	8.0	8.2	8.4	8.2	8.0	8.0	21
Maine	6.7	7.0	7.6	5.9	6.3	6.3	6.5	6.5	7.0	7.1	7.1	42
Maryland	7.0	7.8	7.9	7.0	7.2	7.0	7.3	7.5	7.8	8.0	8.0	21
Massachusetts	6.8	8.0	7.6	6.7	7.3	7.1	7.6	7.9	8.4	8.5	8.5	11
Michigan	4.2	6.4	6.4	5.9	6.8	6.6	7.1	7.3	7.5	7.7	7.7	30
Minnesota	6.7	6.9	7.0	6.2	6.6	6.6	7.0	7.4	7.7	7.9	7.9	27
Mississippi	7.4	7.6	7.4	7.6	7.8	7.6	7.5	7.1	7.7	7.5	7.5	33
Missouri	8.1	8.8	8.8	8.3	8.4	8.4	8.5	8.6	8.7	8.5	8.5	11
Montana	7.3	5.6	5.5	5.5	5.4	5.0	5.1	5.9	6.3	6.3	6.3	50
Nebraska	8.5	8.1	8.4	8.4	8.5	8.6	8.7	8.6	8.9	8.8	8.8	4
Nevada	7.0	7.2	7.4	6.2	7.3	7.4	7.9	8.0	8.5	8.3	8.3	17
New Hampshire	8.2	9.2	8.9	7.4	7.9	8.2	8.5	8.7	9.0	9.1	9.1	1
New Jersey	6.1	7.4	7.9	6.5	6.9	6.5	6.9	7.3	7.8	8.0	8.0	21
New Mexico	8.5	7.9	7.2	7.3	7.5	7.0	7.3	7.4	7.4	7.2	7.2	39
New York	6.0	6.5	6.8	5.1	5.5	5.3	5.9	6.3	7.0	7.1	7.1	42
North Carolina	8.0	8.7	8.7	8.0	8.2	8 0	8.1	8.2	8.4	8.4	8.4	14
North Dakota	8.0	6.7	5.8	5.3	6.1	6.7	6.7	6.2	6.6	6.4	6.4	48
Ohio	5.7	6.6	7.0	5.8	6.2	6.3	6.6	7.0	7.4	7.3	7.3	37
Oklahoma	8.9	8.3	7.9	7.1	7.0	6.9	7.4	7.9	8.1	8.0	8.0	21
Oregon	5.1	5.3	6.8	5.8	6.4	6.2	6.2	6.1	6.9	6.9	6.9	46
Pennsylvania	5.6	6.6	7.4	6.1	6.5	6.4	6.8	7.1	7.5	7.6	7.6	32
Rhode Island	5.3	6.2	6.6	4.0	4.4	4.1	4.8	5.6	6.4	6.4	6.4	48
South Carolina	7.5	8.0	8.4	7.5	7.4	7.5	7.4	7.6	7.9	7.8	7.8	28
South Dakota	7.6	8.4	8.3	8.5	8.5	8.6	8.7	8.8	8.8	8.8	8.8	4
Tennessee	8.1	8.8	8.7	8.5	8.6	8.4	8.4	8.5	8.8	8.8	8.8	4
Texas	10.0	9.2	8.7	8.2	8.3	8.3	8.5	8.7	8.8	8.7	8.7	8
Utah	7.5	7.5	7.2	7.1	7.4	7.6	7.8	7.8	7.9	7.4	7.4	34
Vermont	6.0	6.4	7.2	5.9	6.3	6.1	6.5	6.7	6.9	7.0	7.0	45
Virginia	8.4	8.9	8.9	8.2	8.4	8.3	8.2	8.5	8.7	8.6	8.6	10
Washington	6.4	5.8	6.6	5.5	5.5	4.8	5.5	6.0	6.6	6.5	6.5	47
West Virginia	5.3	4.9	5.3	3.0	4.1	4.9	4.6	4.5	5.2	5.3	5.3	55
Wisconsin	6.6	6.3	7.3	6.9	7.2	7.0	7.3	7.4	7.9	7.7	7.7	30
Wyoming	9.2	7.4	6.8	6.5	6.6	6.6	6.9	7.1	7.1	7.1	7.1	42

* Rank out of 60 for year 2000.

Appendix Table 7: Scores for Area 2 on All-Government Index

	1981	1985	1989	1993	1994	1995	1996	1997	1998	1999	2000	Rank*
Alberta	5.4	5.9	6.0	5.3	5.4	5.4	5.5	5.5	5.4	5.6	6.0	15
British Columbia	4.1	4.4	4.8	3.2	2.9	2.8	2.8	2.9	2.9	3.2	3.4	57
Manitoba	4.3	4.0	4.2	3.1	3.1	3.1	3.4	3.3	3.3	3.2	3.4	57
New Brunswick	2.6	3.9	4.4	3.2	3.0	3.1	3.1	3.2	3.6	3.7	3.9	53
Newfoundland	4.3	3.9	4.2	2.3	2.6	2.4	2.4	2.7	3.0	3.4	3.8	54
Nova Scotia	3.3	3.8	4.6	3.3	3.0	3.2	3.2	3.3	3.4	3.4	3.5	56
Ontario	4.0	4.4	4.4	3.5	3.4	3.4	3.3	3.3	3.6	3.6	4.0	52
Prince Edward Island	4.7	4.8	4.9	3.3	3.3	3.1	3.0	2.9	3.1	3.0	3.1	59
Quebec	3.4	3.3	3.6	2.9	2.8	2.7	2.7	2.6	2.5	2.5	2.9	60
Saskatchewan	3.9	4.4	4.0	2.9	3.1	3.3	3.5	3.4	3.3	3.6	3.7	55
Alabama	4.9	5.4	7.3	6.6	6.2	6.2	6.1	6.0	6.0	6.0	6.0	15
Alaska	6.6	7.0	8.2	6.3	6.4	6.0	6.2	6.0	5.6	6.2	6.2	8
Arizona	4.5	4.8	6.1	5.7	5.6	5.7	5.7	5.7	5.8	5.7	5.9	20
Arkansas	5.3	5.1	7.0	6.2	5.9	5.8	5.6	5.7	5.6	5.4	5.4	37
California	4.9	5.2	7.0	5.8	5.5	5.5	5.5	5.5	5.5	5.7	5.7	26
Colorado	5.3	5.2	6.7	6.5	6.1	6.1	6.2	6.3	6.3	6.3	6.3	4
Connecticut	4.3	5.4	7.2	6.0	5.6	5.4	5.5	5.6	5.5	5.5	5.5	32
Delaware	5.5	5.9	7.9	7.1	6.7	6.9	7.0	7.1	7.0	7.1	7.1	1
Florida	4.7	5.5	6.9	6.0	5.5	5.5	5.4	5.4	5.2	5.2	5.2	43
Georgia	5.2	5.9	7.4	6.7	6.3	6.4	6.3	6.4	6.4	6.3	6.3	4
Hawaii	4.7	5.1	7.1	6.1	5.5	5.4	5.2	5.2	5.3	5.4	5.4	37
Idaho	5.1	4.9	6.5	6.2	5.7	5.7	5.5	5.4	5.4	5.6	5.6	30
Illinois	4.7	5.3	7.0	6.3	6.1	5.9	5.9	6.0	6.1	6.0	6.0	15
Indiana	5.0	5.4	7.3	6.8	6.4	6.4	6.4	6.1	6.3	6.2	6.2	8
Iowa	5.1	4.8	6.6	5.8	5.8	5.6	5.8	5.9	5.7	5.4	5.4	37
Kansas	5.0	5.0	6.6	5.8	5.4	5.4	5.5	5.7	5.5	5.5	5.5	32
Kentucky	5.5	5.7	7.4	6.7	6.3	6.2	6.1	6.0	6.1	6.0	6.0	15
Louisiana	6.8	6.4	7.9	6.8	6.6	6.7	6.6	6.6	6.2	6.1	6.1	12
Maine	4.3	4.6	6.3	5.5	4.9	4.8	4.8	4.5	4.4	4.6	4.6	51
Maryland	4.5	5.1	6.9	5.9	5.5	5.4	5.8	5.7	5.7	5.8	5.8	23
Massachusetts	4.6	5.6	7.3	6.6	6.0	5.9	6.0	6.0	6.0	6.2	6.2	8
Michigan	4.3	4.9	6.6	5.9	5.6	5.6	5.5	5.4	5.6	5.5	5.5	32
Minnesota	4.9	4.9	6.2	5.6	5.2	5.0	5.1	5.1	5.1	5.5	5.5	32
Mississippi	5.0	5.1	6.8	6.4	6.0	5.9	5.7	5.5	5.4	5.3	5.3	40
Missouri	5.3	5.6	7.2	6.7	6.4	6.2	6.3	6.3	6.2	6.1	6.1	12
Montana	5.2	4.5	6.3	5.7	5.1	4.9	4.9	5.0	5.0	5.0	5.0	46
Nebraska	4.9	4.9	6.5	6.0	5.7	5.6	5.8	5.6	5.6	5.7	5.7	26
Nevada	4.9	5.5	7.7	6.7	6.4	6.2	6.3	6.1	6.1	6.0	6.0	15
New Hampshire	4.5	5.9	7.3	5.8	5.9	6.1	6.3	6.3	6.4	6.4	6.4	2
New Jersey	4.1	4.9	6.6	5.6	5.2	5.3	5.3	5.4	5.3	5.3	5.3	40
New Mexico	5.7	5.4	6.2	6.5	6.1	5.8	5.6	5.8	5.4	5.7	5.7	26
New York	4.5	4.7	6.3	5.5	5.1	5.0	5.2	5.3	5.5	5.5	5.5	32
North Carolina	5.3	5.7	7.6	6.8	6.4	6.4	6.4	6.4	6.2	6.3	6.3	4
North Dakota	5.6	4.9	5.7	5.8	5.4	5.2	5.4	5.1	5.1	5.0	5.0	46
Ohio	4.9	4.9	6.6	5.7	5.4	5.3	5.3	5.5	5.6	5.3	5.3	40
Oklahoma	6.0	5.6	6.6	6.3	5.6	5.5	5.6	5.7	5.6	5.6	5.6	30
Oregon	4.4	4.8	6.6	6.3	5.9	5.9	6.1	6.1	6.0	6.1	5.9	20
Pennsylvania	4.6	5.0	6.9	6.3	5.7	5.6	5.6	5.5	5.7	5.7	5.7	26
Rhode Island	3.9	4.2	6.4	5.1	4.5	4.4	4.5	4.9	5.0	4.8	4.8	49
South Carolina	5.0	5.2	7.2	6.3	6.0	6.0	5.9	5.8	5.7	5.8	5.8	23
South Dakota	4.7	5.6	7.3	6.9	6.5	6.4	6.5	6.4	6.0	6.1	6.1	12
Tennessee	4.8	5.6	7.4	6.3	6.5	6.5	6.3	6.3	6.4	6.3	6.3	4
Texas	6.2	6.4	7.5	6.9	6.5	6.5	6.6	6.6	6.5	6.4	6.4	2
Utah	5.0	5.1	6.7	6.4	6.1	6.2	6.4	6.1	6.0	6.0	5.8	23
Vermont	4.5	4.5	6.8	5.7	5.2	5.0	5.0	4.9	4.9	4.9	4.9	48
Virginia	5.0	5.7	7.5	7.0	6.3	6.3	6.3	6.1	6.2	6.2	6.2	8
Washington	4.0	4.5	6.4	5.4	5.1	4.8	4.9	4.9	5.0	5.2	5.2	43
West Virginia	4.5	3.9	6.6	5.5	5.3	5.1	5.1	4.9	4.8	4.8	4.8	49
Wisconsin	4.8	4.5	6.3	5.6	5.3	5.4	5.1	5.3	5.3	5.2	5.2	43
Wyoming	6.5	5.9	7.9	7.2	6.7	6.7	6.6	6.3	6.1	5.9	5.9	20

* Rank out of 60 for year 2000.

Appendix Table 8: Scores for Area 2 on Subnational Index

	1981	1985	1989	1993	1994	1995	1996	1997	1998	1999	2000	Rank*
Alberta	8.1	7.8	7.3	7.0	7.2	7.3	7.4	7.5	7.5	7.6	7.5	10
British Columbia	6.0	5.7	6.1	5.2	5.0	5.0	5.0	5.0	5.2	5.4	5.5	55
Manitoba	6.4	5.5	5.0	4.8	4.8	4.9	5.3	5.1	5.3	5.4	5.4	57
New Brunswick	6.1	5.7	5.5	4.9	5.0	5.1	5.0	5.3	5.6	6.1	6.1	48
Newfoundland	5.7	5.1	5.0	4.2	4.3	4.3	4.3	4.8	5.1	5.4	5.8	52
Nova Scotia	6.2	5.8	5.7	5.2	4.8	5.1	5.4	5.5	5.6	5.9	5.9	51
Ontario	6.8	6.4	5.7	5.2	5.3	5.0	5.3	5.3	5.4	5.8	5.8	52
Prince Edward Island	6.1	5.9	5.9	5.2	4.8	5.0	5.2	5.0	5.1	5.4	5.4	57
Quebec	5.1	4.6	4.7	4.2	4.6	4.2	4.7	4.6	4.4	4.7	4.6	60
Saskatchewan	6.5	6.0	5.1	4.2	4.7	4.8	5.0	4.9	4.9	5.1	5.4	57
Alabama	7.9	7.8	7.7	7.5	7.6	7.5	7.5	7.5	7.5	7.5	7.5	10
Alaska	8.4	8.0	7.7	7.0	7.4	6.8	7.0	6.7	6.5	7.2	7.2	17
Arizona	7.3	6.7	6.0	6.2	6.4	6.5	6.8	7.1	7.0	7.2	7.2	17
Arkansas	7.6	7.1	7.2	7.0	7.0	7.0	6.8	6.7	6.7	6.5	6.5	36
California	6.4	6.3	6.7	6.1	6.2	6.2	6.2	6.3	6.3	6.4	6.4	41
Colorado	8.1	7.2	6.8	7.0	7.0	7.1	7.1	7.2	7.4	7.4	7.4	14
Connecticut	7.8	7.7	7.8	7.0	7.0	6.8	6.8	6.8	6.9	7.1	7.1	23
Delaware	6.7	7.2	7.9	7.8	7.7	7.7	7.9	7.8	7.8	7.9	8.3	1
Florida	8.2	7.7	7.4	7.0	6.9	6.9	6.9	7.0	6.9	7.0	7.0	24
Georgia	7.5	7.5	7.3	7.1	7.1	7.1	7.1	7.2	7.4	7.2	7.2	17
Hawaii	6.1	6.2	6.4	6.1	5.9	5.8	5.6	5.7	5.8	6.2	6.2	47
Idaho	7.0	6.6	6.4	6.3	6.3	6.3	6.1	6.1	6.1	6.3	6.3	45
Illinois	7.7	7.6	7.7	7.3	7.4	7.2	7.3	7.4	7.5	7.4	7.4	14
Indiana	8.1	7.5	7.5	7.8	7.7	7.6	7.8	7.5	7.7	7.7	7.7	4
Iowa	7.8	6.8	6.7	6.5	6.7	6.6	6.8	6.9	7.1	6.9	6.9	27
Kansas	6.8	6.5	7.0	6.3	6.2	6.3	6.4	6.5	6.7	6.8	6.8	31
Kentucky	7.7	7.5	7.3	7.2	7.2	7.1	7.0	7.0	7.1	7.0	7.0	24
Louisiana	9.1	8.0	7.8	7.6	7.8	7.8	7.7	7.6	7.3	7.3	7.3	16
Maine	6.0	6.0	6.1	5.6	5.7	5.6	5.7	5.3	5.2	5.5	5.5	55
Maryland	7.4	7.4	7.5	7.1	7.2	7.1	7.3	7.2	7.2	7.5	7.5	10
Massachusetts	7.2	7.7	7.7	7.4	7.4	7.3	7.4	7.4	7.6	7.7	7.7	4
Michigan	6.7	6.9	6.8	6.6	6.9	7.1	7.1	6.9	7.1	7.0	7.0	24
Minnesota	5.7	6.2	6.2	6.1	6.3	6.0	6.2	6.2	6.2	6.4	6.4	41
Mississippi	7.4	6.9	6.8	6.7	6.7	6.6	6.5	6.5	6.4	6.3	6.3	45
Missouri	7.7	7.4	7.4	7.7	7.8	7.5	7.6	7.6	7.6	7.6	7.6	7
Montana	7.7	6.6	6.1	6.4	6.3	6.2	6.3	6.3	6.4	6.5	6.5	36
Nebraska	6.3	6.4	6.8	6.5	6.5	6.5	6.5	6.4	6.5	6.8	6.8	31
Nevada	7.6	7.2	7.5	7.1	7.3	7.0	7.1	7.1	7.2	7.2	7.2	17
New Hampshire	8.0	8.2	8.0	6.3	7.5	7.6	7.8	8.0	8.1	8.1	8.1	2
New Jersey	7.4	7.3	7.3	6.7	6.5	6.4	6.4	6.6	6.6	6.7	6.7	34
New Mexico	7.5	6.9	6.1	6.6	6.7	6.5	6.3	6.5	6.2	6.4	6.4	41
New York	5.1	5.1	6.1	5.7	5.7	5.7	6.0	6.1	6.3	6.4	6.4	41
North Carolina	7.5	7.4	7.5	7.1	7.1	7.1	7.1	7.2	7.0	7.2	7.2	17
North Dakota	8.4	6.5	5.4	6.6	6.7	6.5	6.7	6.4	6.5	6.5	6.5	36
Ohio	7.8	6.4	6.9	6.3	6.4	6.3	6.3	6.7	6.9	6.6	6.6	35
Oklahoma	8.0	7.3	6.8	7.3	6.7	6.6	6.7	6.7	6.6	6.8	6.8	31
Oregon	7.1	6.8	6.6	7.0	7.3	7.3	7.3	7.4	7.5	7.6	6.9	27
Pennsylvania	7.7	7.5	7.7	7.4	7.4	7.3	7.4	7.2	7.5	7.5	7.5	10
Rhode Island	5.7	6.0	6.9	5.9	5.5	5.5	5.6	5.7	5.9	6.0	6.0	50
South Carolina	7.3	7.1	7.0	6.8	6.9	6.8	6.9	6.8	6.8	6.9	6.9	27
South Dakota	7.6	7.6	7.5	7.7	7.7	7.6	7.7	7.7	7.4	7.6	7.6	7
Tennessee	8.0	7.8	7.8	6.7	7.7	7.8	7.7	7.7	7.8	7.8	7.8	3
Texas	9.0	8.3	7.7	7.6	7.6	7.7	7.7	7.7	7.8	7.7	7.7	4
Utah	7.7	6.8	6.5	6.6	6.9	7.0	7.2	7.0	7.0	7.1	6.9	27
Vermont	5.3	5.6	6.8	6.0	6.0	5.9	5.9	5.9	6.0	6.1	6.1	48
Virginia	7.7	7.8	7.7	7.6	7.6	7.5	7.6	7.5	7.5	7.6	7.6	7
Washington	7.1	6.4	6.4	6.1	6.2	5.8	5.9	6.1	6.3	6.5	6.5	36
West Virginia	5.7	4.9	6.6	6.1	6.2	6.1	6.2	5.9	5.9	5.8	5.8	52
Wisconsin	6.6	6.0	6.4	6.2	6.1	6.3	6.0	6.2	6.2	6.2	6.5	36
Wyoming	8.4	7.1	7.5	7.8	7.7	7.7	7.6	7.5	7.3	7.2	7.2	17

* Rank out of 60 for year 2000.

Appendix Table 9: Scores for Area 3 on All-Government Index

	1981	1985	1989	1993	1994	1995	1996	1997	1998	1999	2000	Rank*
Alberta	4.0	4.2	4.3	4.7	5.1	5.3	5.6	5.9	5.8	5.8	6.1	47
British Columbia	4.0	4.0	4.4	4.0	4.1	3.8	3.8	4.0	3.9	4.1	4.0	56
Manitoba	2.7	2.7	2.9	2.7	2.8	2.9	3.1	3.4	3.5	3.2	3.4	58
New Brunswick	1.8	2.5	3.3	3.4	3.6	3.9	3.8	3.9	4.1	4.3	4.4	55
Newfoundland	2.5	2.8	4.1	4.2	4.6	4.9	4.7	4.7	5.0	5.6	5.8	52
Nova Scotia	1.3	2.8	4.0	4.5	4.9	5.2	5.3	5.4	5.7	5.9	6.0	49
Ontario	4.7	4.7	4.8	3.9	4.0	4.1	4.3	4.5	4.6	4.8	4.9	54
Prince Edward Island	3.5	3.0	2.9	2.6	2.5	2.7	2.6	2.5	2.7	3.1	3.3	60
Quebec	1.5	2.2	2.7	2.3	2.4	2.4	2.6	2.7	2.9	3.2	3.4	58
Saskatchewan	2.8	3.0	3.2	3.0	3.2	3.4	3.5	3.6	3.6	3.5	3.7	57
Alabama	8.0	8.2	8.3	8.4	8.4	8.5	8.6	8.6	8.6	8.6	8.6	1
Alaska	6.6	6.7	6.6	6.3	6.4	6.5	6.6	6.5	6.4	6.5	6.6	35
Arizona	7.6	7.9	7.9	7.7	7.8	7.9	7.9	8.0	8.1	8.1	8.1	4
Arkansas	5.1	5.4	5.8	5.9	5.9	6.0	6.1	6.1	5.8	5.9	6.0	49
California	6.0	6.6	6.7	6.6	6.7	6.7	6.8	6.8	6.8	6.9	7.0	26
Colorado	7.8	7.7	7.9	8.2	8.4	8.5	8.6	8.2	8.2	8.3	8.4	2
Connecticut	6.6	7.4	7.6	7.8	7.9	8.0	8.1	8.0	8.0	8.0	8.1	4
Delaware	7.2	7.5	7.8	7.8	7.9	8.0	8.0	8.0	8.0	8.1	8.1	4
Florida	7.8	7.9	7.8	7.6	7.6	7.7	7.7	7.7	7.8	7.8	7.8	11
Georgia	6.7	6.2	6.6	6.7	6.8	6.9	7.1	7.1	7.2	7.3	7.4	20
Hawaii	5.9	6.3	6.8	6.6	6.6	6.7	6.7	6.7	6.7	6.8	6.8	32
Idaho	5.6	6.1	5.8	6.1	6.3	6.4	6.5	6.5	6.3	6.4	6.5	37
Illinois	6.6	6.7	6.8	6.8	6.9	7.0	7.1	7.0	7.0	7.0	7.1	24
Indiana	7.0	7.5	7.2	7.5	7.7	7.8	7.8	7.9	8.0	8.0	8.0	8
Iowa	7.8	7.7	5.8	5.9	6.0	6.1	6.2	6.3	6.2	6.2	6.3	44
Kansas	6.9	7.1	6.8	6.8	6.9	7.0	7.0	7.2	7.2	7.3	7.3	22
Kentucky	6.3	6.4	6.1	6.0	6.1	6.2	6.3	6.4	6.5	6.5	6.6	35
Louisiana	8.1	7.9	7.8	7.7	7.7	7.7	7.7	7.8	7.8	7.8	7.8	11
Maine	4.6	5.5	5.9	5.8	5.9	6.0	6.1	6.0	6.0	6.1	6.2	46
Maryland	4.3	5.3	5.8	5.7	5.8	5.9	6.0	5.9	5.9	6.0	6.1	47
Massachusetts	5.9	6.9	7.2	7.2	7.3	7.3	7.3	7.2	7.3	7.4	7.5	17
Michigan	6.2	7.1	7.4	7.6	7.8	7.8	7.9	8.0	7.5	7.6	7.6	16
Minnesota	6.1	6.5	6.5	6.7	6.8	6.9	7.0	7.1	7.0	7.1	7.1	24
Mississippi	7.9	7.9	7.8	7.8	7.8	7.8	7.8	7.8	7.8	7.8	7.8	11
Missouri	9.0	9.0	7.4	7.3	7.4	7.5	7.6	7.5	7.4	7.5	7.5	17
Montana	5.9	5.6	5.3	5.5	5.6	5.7	5.8	5.7	5.7	5.7	5.8	52
Nebraska	6.8	7.0	6.5	6.5	6.6	6.7	6.8	6.9	6.7	6.8	6.9	29
Nevada	7.3	7.6	7.7	7.6	7.7	7.8	7.9	7.8	7.8	7.8	7.9	10
New Hampshire	5.7	6.7	6.7	6.5	6.6	6.7	6.8	6.7	6.7	6.8	6.9	29
New Jersey	6.1	6.9	7.1	6.8	6.8	6.9	7.0	7.1	7.1	7.2	7.3	22
New Mexico	5.4	5.5	5.6	6.1	5.9	6.0	6.1	6.2	6.2	6.2	6.3	44
New York	5.6	6.2	6.4	6.4	6.5	6.6	6.7	6.7	6.8	6.9	6.9	29
North Carolina	5.6	6.1	6.6	6.4	6.5	6.6	6.6	6.7	6.5	6.6	6.7	33
North Dakota	5.7	5.7	5.6	5.6	5.8	5.9	6.1	5.9	5.9	5.9	6.0	49
Ohio	6.3	6.8	6.4	6.4	6.6	6.7	6.7	6.8	6.9	7.0	7.0	26
Oklahoma	6.5	6.4	6.1	6.1	6.2	6.3	6.5	6.4	6.3	6.4	6.5	37
Oregon	5.4	5.9	5.6	5.9	6.1	6.2	6.4	6.3	6.2	6.3	6.4	42
Pennsylvania	6.5	7.1	7.4	7.5	7.6	7.7	7.7	7.7	7.7	7.7	7.8	11
Rhode Island	5.5	6.1	6.2	6.3	6.3	6.4	6.5	6.4	6.5	6.6	6.7	33
South Carolina	8.0	8.1	8.1	8.0	8.0	8.1	8.1	8.2	8.2	8.2	8.1	4
South Dakota	7.1	7.2	7.2	7.5	7.7	7.8	8.0	8.0	7.8	7.9	8.0	8
Tennessee	7.7	7.9	8.0	8.0	8.1	8.1	8.1	8.1	8.2	8.2	8.2	3
Texas	7.5	7.5	6.5	6.6	6.6	6.6	6.7	6.8	6.9	6.9	7.0	26
Utah	5.4	5.9	5.6	5.8	6.0	6.1	6.3	6.2	6.2	6.3	6.4	42
Vermont	6.4	7.2	7.5	7.3	7.4	7.3	7.3	7.3	7.3	7.4	7.5	17
Virginia	5.4	6.2	6.6	6.0	6.1	6.2	6.3	6.3	6.3	6.4	6.5	37
Washington	6.3	6.5	6.0	6.1	6.2	6.0	6.1	6.2	6.3	6.4	6.5	37
West Virginia	5.9	6.0	6.3	6.1	6.2	6.4	6.4	6.5	6.3	6.4	6.5	37
Wisconsin	6.3	6.8	7.0	7.1	7.2	7.3	7.4	7.3	7.3	7.4	7.4	20
Wyoming	7.9	7.5	7.3	7.4	7.5	7.6	7.6	7.7	7.7	7.7	7.8	11

* Rank out of 60 for year 2000.

Appendix Table 10: Scores for Area 3 on Subnational Index

	1981	1985	1989	1993	1994	1995	1996	1997	1998	1999	2000	Rank*
Alberta	3.8	4.0	4.1	4.3	4.7	5.0	5.2	5.6	5.5	5.5	5.8	51
British Columbia	3.8	3.9	4.3	3.8	4.0	3.7	3.6	3.8	3.8	3.9	3.9	56
Manitoba	3.1	3.0	3.1	2.8	2.9	3.0	3.1	3.2	3.3	3.0	3.2	59
New Brunswick	1.9	2.5	3.2	3.4	3.6	3.9	3.8	3.8	4.0	4.2	4.3	55
Newfoundland	2.5	2.7	3.9	4.0	4.3	4.6	4.5	4.4	4.7	5.3	5.6	53
Nova Scotia	1.6	3.0	4.1	4.5	4.8	5.2	5.2	5.4	5.6	5.8	5.9	49
Ontario	4.7	4.8	4.8	3.9	3.9	4.0	4.2	4.5	4.7	4.9	5.0	54
Prince Edward Island	3.4	3.0	2.8	2.6	2.6	2.8	2.7	2.6	2.8	3.1	3.3	58
Quebec	1.2	2.0	2.4	2.0	2.0	2.1	2.3	2.5	2.7	3.0	3.2	59
Saskatchewan	2.8	2.9	3.1	2.8	3.0	3.2	3.3	3.5	3.4	3.2	3.4	57
Alabama	8.2	8.4	8.4	8.4	8.5	8.5	8.6	8.6	8.6	8.6	8.6	1
Alaska	7.1	7.0	6.9	6.7	6.8	6.8	6.9	6.8	6.6	6.7	6.8	30
Arizona	7.7	7.9	7.9	7.7	7.8	7.9	7.9	8.0	8.1	8.1	8.1	3
Arkansas	5.1	5.4	5.8	5.8	5.8	6.0	6.0	6.0	5.7	5.8	5.9	49
California	6.1	6.7	6.7	6.6	6.7	6.7	6.8	6.7	6.7	6.8	6.9	27
Colorado	7.9	7.8	8.0	8.3	8.5	8.5	8.6	8.2	8.2	8.3	8.4	2
Connecticut	6.6	7.4	7.6	7.8	7.8	7.9	8.0	8.0	7.9	8.0	8.0	6
Delaware	7.1	7.4	7.8	7.8	7.8	7.9	7.9	7.9	7.9	8.0	8.0	6
Florida	7.8	7.9	7.8	7.6	7.6	7.6	7.7	7.7	7.7	7.8	7.8	11
Georgia	6.8	6.3	6.7	6.8	6.9	7.0	7.1	7.2	7.2	7.3	7.4	19
Hawaii	6.5	6.9	7.3	7.0	7.0	7.0	7.0	7.0	7.0	7.1	7.1	24
Idaho	5.7	6.1	5.8	6.0	6.3	6.4	6.4	6.5	6.2	6.3	6.5	37
Illinois	6.6	6.7	6.8	6.8	6.9	6.9	7.0	7.0	6.9	7.0	7.0	25
Indiana	6.9	7.4	7.2	7.5	7.6	7.7	7.7	7.8	7.9	7.9	8.0	6
Iowa	7.7	7.6	5.6	5.7	5.9	5.9	6.1	6.1	6.0	6.1	6.1	47
Kansas	6.8	7.1	6.7	6.7	6.7	6.8	6.9	7.0	7.1	7.1	7.2	22
Kentucky	6.4	6.5	6.1	6.0	6.1	6.2	6.3	6.4	6.4	6.5	6.5	37
Louisiana	8.0	7.7	7.7	7.5	7.5	7.5	7.6	7.6	7.6	7.6	7.6	13
Maine	4.8	5.6	6.0	5.8	5.9	6.0	6.1	6.0	6.0	6.1	6.2	46
Maryland	5.0	6.0	6.4	6.3	6.4	6.4	6.5	6.4	6.4	6.5	6.5	37
Massachusetts	5.9	6.9	7.2	7.2	7.3	7.3	7.3	7.2	7.3	7.4	7.5	16
Michigan	6.1	6.9	7.3	7.4	7.6	7.7	7.8	7.8	7.4	7.5	7.5	16
Minnesota	5.9	6.4	6.4	6.6	6.7	6.8	6.9	7.0	6.9	6.9	7.0	25
Mississippi	7.9	7.8	7.7	7.7	7.7	7.7	7.7	7.7	7.7	7.7	7.6	13
Missouri	9.1	9.2	7.5	7.4	7.5	7.6	7.6	7.5	7.4	7.5	7.5	16
Montana	6.1	5.7	5.4	5.6	5.7	5.8	5.8	5.7	5.7	5.8	5.8	51
Nebraska	6.7	6.9	6.5	6.4	6.5	6.6	6.7	6.8	6.6	6.7	6.8	30
Nevada	7.3	7.7	7.7	7.6	7.8	7.8	7.9	7.8	7.7	7.8	7.9	9
New Hampshire	5.7	6.7	6.7	6.4	6.5	6.6	6.7	6.6	6.7	6.7	6.8	30
New Jersey	6.1	6.9	7.1	6.7	6.8	6.8	6.9	7.0	7.0	7.1	7.2	22
New Mexico	5.7	5.7	5.7	6.1	6.0	6.1	6.1	6.2	6.2	6.2	6.3	44
New York	5.5	6.1	6.3	6.3	6.3	6.5	6.6	6.6	6.7	6.7	6.8	30
North Carolina	5.5	6.1	6.5	6.3	6.4	6.5	6.5	6.6	6.4	6.5	6.6	36
North Dakota	5.8	5.7	5.6	5.6	5.8	5.9	6.1	5.9	5.9	5.9	6.1	47
Ohio	6.3	6.7	6.4	6.4	6.5	6.6	6.7	6.8	6.8	6.9	6.9	27
Oklahoma	6.6	6.5	6.2	6.1	6.2	6.3	6.5	6.4	6.3	6.4	6.5	37
Oregon	5.4	5.9	5.6	5.9	6.0	6.2	6.4	6.3	6.2	6.2	6.3	44
Pennsylvania	6.6	7.2	7.6	7.6	7.7	7.7	7.8	7.7	7.7	7.8	7.8	11
Rhode Island	5.5	6.1	6.3	6.3	6.4	6.5	6.5	6.4	6.5	6.6	6.7	34
South Carolina	8.0	8.1	8.1	7.9	7.9	7.9	8.0	8.0	8.0	8.0	7.9	9
South Dakota	7.2	7.3	7.3	7.6	7.8	7.9	8.0	8.1	7.9	8.0	8.1	3
Tennessee	7.9	8.0	8.1	8.0	8.1	8.1	8.1	8.1	8.1	8.1	8.1	3
Texas	7.6	7.5	6.5	6.5	6.5	6.5	6.6	6.8	6.8	6.9	6.9	27
Utah	5.8	6.3	5.9	5.9	6.1	6.2	6.4	6.3	6.2	6.3	6.4	41
Vermont	6.3	7.1	7.4	7.3	7.3	7.2	7.2	7.2	7.3	7.3	7.4	19
Virginia	6.0	6.7	7.1	6.5	6.5	6.6	6.7	6.6	6.6	6.7	6.7	34
Washington	6.4	6.6	6.1	6.1	6.2	6.0	6.1	6.2	6.3	6.4	6.4	41
West Virginia	5.8	5.8	6.2	6.0	6.1	6.3	6.3	6.4	6.3	6.4	6.4	41
Wisconsin	6.1	6.6	6.9	7.0	7.1	7.2	7.3	7.2	7.2	7.2	7.3	21
Wyoming	7.9	7.3	7.2	7.3	7.4	7.4	7.5	7.5	7.6	7.6	7.6	13

* Rank out of 60 for year 2000.

Appendix C: Methodology

To avoid subjective judgments, objective methods were used to calculate and weight the variables. For all variables, each observation was transformed into a number from zero to 10 using the following formula: $(V_{max} - V_i) / (V_{max} - V_{min}) \times 10$, where V_{max} is the largest value found within a variable, V_{min} is the smallest, and V_i is the observation to be transformed. For each variable, the mini-max calculation included all data for all years to allow comparisons over time.

To transform the individual variables into areas and overall summary indexes, Areas 1, 2, and 3 were equally weighted, and each of the variables within each area was equally weighted. For example, the weight for Area 1 was 33.3%. Area 1 has two variables, each of which received equal weight in calculating Area 1, or 16.7% in calculating the overall index.

Calculating the income tax variable was more complicated. The variable examining the top marginal income tax rate and income threshold at which it applies was transformed into a score from zero to 10 using matrix 1 and matrix 2. Canadian nominal thresholds were first converted into constant 2000 Canadian dollars by using the implicit chain price index and then converted into US dollars using the average US/Canada exchange rate for each year. US nominal thresholds were converted into real 2000 US dollars using the Chain-type Quantity Index. This procedure is based on the transformation system found in *Economic Freedom of the World: 1975–1995* (Gwartney et al. 1996), modified for this study to take into account a different range of top marginal tax rates and income thresholds.

Matrix 1 was used in calculating the score for Area 2B, Top Marginal Income Tax Rate and the Income Threshold at Which It Applies, at an all-government level; matrix 2 was used to calculate the score for Area 2B at a subnational level.

In setting the threshold levels for income taxes at the subnational level, we faced an interesting quandary. In the United States, state thresholds were, with rare exceptions, below US federal thresholds. In Canada, provincial thresholds were frequently higher than federal thresholds. Whenever the provincial or state threshold was higher than the federal threshold, the federal threshold was used at a subnational level since, when a provincial threshold is above the national level, the cause is typically the imposition of a relatively small surcharge on high-income earners. Because of the structure of these matrixes, this can produce perverse scoring results. For example, in matrix 2 a jurisdiction gets a score of 2.5 if it has a marginal income tax rate of, say, 12.5% for incomes over $50,000. Let's say the jurisdiction imposes a surcharge for income earners above $100,000, increasing the marginal rate to 13%. In matrix 2, even though additional taxes in the form of a surcharge have been imposed, the state's score perversely increases to 3 because of the increase in the threshold level.

Our decision to use the federal threshold as the default threshold when the provincial threshold was higher is, frankly, a matter of judgement. Thus, it was important to understand whether this would affect the results significantly. To see whether this was so, we calculated the overall index both ways and found that changes were small and that the overall results were not affected. (Results of the tests are posted on our website, www.freetheworld.com.)

Matrix 1: Income Tax Matrix for Area 2B: All-Government Level

	Income Threshold Level (2000US$)		
Top Marginal Tax Rate	Less than $50,000	$50,000 to $100,000	More than $100,000
27% or less	10.0	10.0	10.0
27% to 30%[2]	9.0	9.5	10.0
30% to 33%	8.0	8.5	9.0
33% to 36%	7.0	7.5	8.0
36% to 39%	6.0	6.5	7.0
39% to 42%	5.0	5.5	6.0
42% to 45%	4.0	4.5	5.0
45% to 48%	3.0	3.5	4.0
48% to 51%	2.0	2.5	3.0
51% to 54%	1.0	1.5	2.0
54% to 57%	0.0	0.5	1.0
57% to 60%	0.0	0.0	0.5
60% or more	0.0	0.0	0.0

Matrix 2: Income Tax Matrix for Area 2B: Subnational Level

	Income Threshold Level (US$2000)		
Top Marginal Tax Rate	Less than $50,000	$50,000 to $100,000	More than $100,000
1.5% or less	10.0	10.0	10.0
1.5% to 3.0%	9.0	9.5	10.0
3.0% to 4.5%	8.0	8.5	9.0
4.5% to 6.0%	7.0	7.5	8.0
6.0% to 7.5%	6.0	6.5	7.0
7.5% to 9.0%	5.0	5.5	6.0
9.0% to 10.5%	4.0	4.5	5.0
10.5% to 12.0%	3.0	3.5	4.0
12.0% to 13.5%	2.0	2.5	3.0
13.5% to 15.0%	1.0	1.5	2.0
15.0% to 16.5%	0.0	0.5	1.0
16.5% to 18.0%	0.0	0.0	0.5
18.0 %or more	0.0	0.0	0.0

Note: The range is actually from 27.00% to 29.99% but for convenience we have written it as "27% to 30%." This applies to all other marginal tax-rate ranges in matrix 1 and matrix 2 as well.

Appendix D: Adjustment Factors

Due to constitutional differences and differences in policy, in the United States, subnational jurisdictions take a proportionately smaller share of overall government spending than in Canada. In 1999, for instance, provinces and local governments accounted for about 78% of government consumption in Canada, while, in the United States, state and local government are responsible for 73% of government consumption, just 93% of the level in Canada to be precise: 0.73/0.78 = 0.93. This is what we term the adjustment factor or, put more precisely, R_U/R_C, where R_U is the percent of total government spending at the state level in the United States, and R_C is the percent of total government spending at the provincial level in Canada. Because of this difference in government structure in the United States and Canada, a direct comparison would not be appropriate. Instead, we use this adjustment factor, multiplying provincial and local government consumption in Canada by 0.93 so that it will be comparable to United States data.

At the subnational level, similar adjustment factors are calculated for each year for each variable in Areas 1 and 2 as well as for variable 3B: Government Employment as a Percentage of Total State/Provincial Employment. For example, the adjustment factor for 2A: Total Government Revenue from Own Source as a Percentage of GDP, at a subnational level is calculated as average total government revenue at a state level as a percentage of average total government revenue at all-government levels in the United States divided by average total government revenue at a provincial level as a percentage of average total government revenue at all-government level in Canada.

No adjustment factor is necessary at the all-government level because every level of government is counted. Note that 2D: Sales Tax as a Percentage of GDP is not adjusted because the United States does not have a federal sales tax and Canada does.

We faced another common problem in comparing statistics across time, changes in the structure of some series over time. Similarly, some spending categories were not strictly comparable between Canada and the United States. This required the use of judgment in some cases. Fortunately, with one exception, these problems arose with minor-subcomponents of variables which typically represent only 1% or 2% of the overall size of the variable. The exception was accounting for medical care spending, which is structured as government consumption in Canada and as a set of transfer programs in the United States. Given that the index captures the impact of both government consumption and of transfer programs, we decided the most accurate method of accounting was to reflect the actual nature of the spending, a transfer program in the United States and government consumption in Canada, rather than artificially include one or other in an inappropriate variable.

A further complication arose in applying the adjustment factor to the income tax variable at the sub-national level. To construct this adjustment factor, the Canadian top marginal tax rates at a subnational level are multiplied by the ratio of average personal tax revenue at a state level as a percentage of average personal tax revenue at an all-government level in US and average personal tax revenue at a provincial level as a percentage of average personal tax revenue at an all-government level in Canada. For example, in 1999, in Canada, provinces collected 39.40% of the income tax revenue raised in Canada. In the United States, states collected 18.35% of all income taxes. Thus, 18.35/39.40 equals 46.57%. In Ontario, the top marginal rate in 1999 was 17.87%. This is reduced to 8.32% when the adjustment factor is applied.

Appendix E: Explanation of the Variables & Data Sources

Area 1. Size of Government

1A. General Consumption Expenditures by Government as a Percentage of GDP

The Canadian data at a subnational and all-government level are from the Provincial Economic Accounts, Statistics Canada. General consumption expenditure at a provincial and local (subnational) level is defined as net current expenditure by provincial and local governments (i.e., total expenditures minus transfers to persons, transfers to businesses, transfers to other governments, and interest on public debt). At an all-government level, consumption expenditure is defined as net current expenditure by federal, provincial, and local governments where the definition of net expenditure is the same as at a subnational level. In order to account for the different split of responsibilities between the federal and other levels of government in Canada and the United States, an adjustment factor was applied to the Canadian data (see Appendix D: Adjustment Factors for more information).

The US data for general consumption expenditures at a state and local level are from the US Census Bureau (various files available online http://www.census.gov/govs/www/estimate.html). The 1980's data are from US Census Bureau "ftp" files (ftp://ftp.census.gov/pub/outgoing/). General government consumption expenditures at a state and local level are defined as other direct general expenditures minus welfare (i.e., total expenditures minus expenditures on utilities, insurance trust—worker's compensation and employment insurance—capital outlays, and direct—not intergovernmental—public welfare payments). The data for government expenditures at a federal level are from *Facts and Figures on Government Finance,* The Tax Foundation (various issues) from 1981 to 1997. The data from 1998 to 2000 are from the *Consolidated Federal Funds Report,* US Census Bureau (various issues). General consumption expenditure at an all-government level is defined as consumption expenditure at a state and local level plus federal consumption expenditure (i.e., federal salaries and wages plus federal procurement).

1B: Transfers and Subsidies as a Percentage of GDP

The Canadian data for transfers at a subnational and all government level are from Provincial Economic Accounts, Statistics Canada. Transfers are defined as current transfers to persons and businesses.

The US data for transfers at a state and local level are from the US Census Bureau "ftp" files (ftp://ftp.census.gov/pub/outgoing/). At a subnational level, transfers are defined as total insurance trust benefits (expenditures) plus total assistance and subsidies minus total retirement expenditures. At an all-government level, transfers are calculated as total transfer payments by federal, state, and local governments to persons and businesses. The data for transfers at an all-government level are from the Bureau of Economic Analysis (http://www.bea.doc.gov/bea/regional/spi).

Area 2: Takings and Discriminatory Taxation

2A: Total Government Revenue from Own Source as a Percentage of GDP

The Canadian data, at a subnational level, are from Financial Management System, Public Institutions Division, Statistics Canada. At a subnational level, own source revenue is defined as a sum of income taxes, consumption taxes, property and other taxes, health insurance premiums, contributions to social insurance plans, taxes from sales of goods and services, investment income, and other own-source revenue. The data for own-source revenue at an all-government level are from Provincial Economic Accounts, Statistics Canada. At an all-government level, own-source revenue is defined as a sum of direct taxes from persons, direct taxes from businesses, taxes from non-residents, contributions to social insurance plans, indirect taxes, other transfers from persons and investment income.

The US data at a subnational level are from US Census Bureau "ftp" files (ftp://ftp.census.gov/pub/outgoing/). Own-source revenue at a subnational level is calculated as general state and local own-source revenue plus insurance trust, liquor store, and utility revenue. Own-source revenue at an all-government level is calculated as own-source revenue at a subnational level plus own-source revenue at a federal level. The data for the federal own-source revenue are from *Facts and Figures on Government Finance*, The Tax Foundation (various issues).

2B: Top Marginal Income Tax Rate and the Income Threshold at Which It Applies

The Canadian data at a subnational and all-government level are from the *Finances of the Nation*, Canadian Tax Foundation (various issues). Thresholds are first converted into 2000 Canadian dollars using GDP implicit chain price deflator from CANSIM, Statistics Canada (Table 380-0056). Then the thresholds were transformed into US currency using the average exchange rate for the appropriate year retrieved from the Pacific Exchange Rate Service (pacific.commerce.ubc.ca/xr/data.html).

The US data are from *Facts and Figures on Government Finances*, The Tax Foundation (various issues). The federal tax rates, for some of the years, are from Internal Revenue Service , Department of the Treasury (various issues). Some of the data for state top marginal tax rates and thresholds at which these rates apply are from *Significant Features of Fiscal Federalism*, Advisory Commission on Intergovernmental Relations (various issues), and Federation of Tax Administrators web site (http://www.taxadmin.org). Threshold are converted into 2000 US dollars using Quantity index for Real GSP from the Bureau of Economic Analysis (available at www.bea.doc.gov).

2C: Indirect Taxes as a Percentage of GDP

The Canadian data at a subnational and all-government level are from Provincial Economic Accounts, Statistics Canada. Indirect tax revenue at a subnational level is defined as total indirect tax revenue plus employer contributions to worker's compensation minus sales tax revenue. Indirect tax revenue at an all-government level is defined as indirect tax revenue at a subnational level plus federal indirect tax, employer and employee contributions to employment insurance, employer and employee contributions to Canada Pension Plan (plus employer and employee contributions to Quebec Pension Plan for Quebec) minus federal sales tax revenue.

The US data at a subnational level are from US Census Bureau "ftp" files (ftp://ftp.census.gov/pub/outgoing/). Indirect tax revenue at a subnational level is defined as the sum of property tax, total selective sales tax, total license tax, liquor store revenue, unemployment payroll tax, and total worker compensation revenue minus the alcohol beverage and tobacco tax revenue at a state and local level. The data at a federal level are from *Facts and Figures on Government Finances*, Tax Foundation (various issues). The indirect tax at an all-government level is defined as indirect tax at a subnational level plus social insurance, custom duties, airport trust fund, highway trust fund, other excise, and estate and gift tax revenue at a federal level.

2D: Sales Taxes Collected as a Percentage of GDP

The Canadian data at a subnational and all-government level are from Provincial Economic Accounts, Statistics Canada. Sales tax at a subnational and all-government level is defined as retail sales tax revenue at local and provincial level and local, provincial, and federal level respectively.

The US data at a subnational level are from US Census Bureau "ftp" files (ftp://ftp.census.gov/pub/outgoing/). The sales tax is defined as a general sales tax revenue. Note that the Unied States does not have a federal sales tax.

Area 3: Labor Market Freedom

3A: Minimum Wage Legislation

Provincial minimum wage data are from Human Resources Development Canada (http://206.191.16.130/psait_spila/lmnec_eslc/eslc/salaire_minwage/report2/report2_e.cfm). This variable was calculated as minimum wage multiplied by 2,080, which is the full-time equivalent measure of work hours per year (52 weeks multiplied by 40 hours per week) as a percentage of per-capita GDP.

US minimum wage data are from *The Book of the States,* Council of State Governments (various issues) and the *Monthly Labor Review,* Bureau of Labor Statistics (stats.bls.gov/opub/mlr/mlrhome.htm). Note that federal minimum wage is not used at an all-government level; the minimum wage at state or provincial level is used instead because the federal minimum wage applies to a very small percentage of working population.

3B: Government Employment as a Percentage of Total State/Provincial Employment

The Canadian data at a subnational and all-government level are from Provincial Economic Accounts, Statistics Canada (total employment data) and from Financial Management System, Public Institutions Division, Statistics Canada (government employment data).

The US data for government employment and total state employment are from the US Census Bureau (www.bea.doc.gov). Note that neither the United States nor Canadian government employment at a federal level includes military employment.

3C: Occupational Licensing

Canadian information was found in *Occupational Regulation in Canada* by Evans and Stanbury and updated by Faisal Arman using provincial statute records. The US information was from *The Book of the States* (various issues) and the *Directory of Professional and Occupational Regulation in the United States and Canada,* CLEAR.

The occupational licensing variable does not look exhaustively at the number of regulated occupations but rather at a subset of occupations. To be included in this subset, the occupation needs to be regulated in at least one case in both Canada and the United States. This was done because the US data was more extensive and comprehensive, with multiple subprofessionals being recorded as regulated. If each subprofession were counted, this would tend to inflate the US numbers but it would not be accurate to claim that more occupations were regulated than in Canada. Another unfortunate complication is that the data for the early time period are less complete than the later information. The assumption used to compute a score, which would tend to bias the results, is that any occupation that does not have information recorded for it in the early period was regulated similarly as it was in the later period.

Data Sources for Other Variables

The Gross Domestic Product and population data for Canadian provinces are from Provincial Economic Accounts, Statistics Canada. The implicit chained price index was used to transform the nominal GDP into real GDP values. After the Canadian per-capita GDP was deflated, it was transformed in US dollars using the exchange rate from Pacific Exchange Rate Service (http://pacific.commerce.ubc.ca/xr/data.html).

The US Gross State Product and population data are from the Bureau of Economic Analysis (http://www.bea.doc.gov). The GSP deflator (Quantity Index for Real GSP) from the Bureau of Economic Analysis (http://www.bea.doc.gov/bea/regional/gsp/action.cfm) was used to transform nominal GSP values into real US dollars.

The Canadian data for high school graduates as a percentage of population (25 years old and older) are from two sources. The data on high school graduates are from Catalogue #81-229-Education, Statistics Canada. Note that the Canadian data include public, private, and federal schools and schools for visually and hearing impaired as well as schools overseas. The data on population 25 years and older are from Statistics Canada on line (CANSIM label numbers are D985116, D985398, D985680, D985962, D986244, D986526, D986808, D987090, D987372, and D987654).

The data on US public high school graduates are from the Statistical Abstract of the United States (various issues) for the period from 1981 to 1993. From 1993 to 2000, data on public high school graduates are from National Center for Education Statistics, US Department of Education (http://nces.ed.gov/quicktables). Private high-school graduates data are from Statistical Abstract of the United States for 1981 and from *Private High School Survey*, National Center for Education Statistics, US Department of Education (various issues) from 1985 to 2000. The data on population 25 years and older are from Population Division, the US Census Bureau (http://eire.census.gov/popest/archives/1990.php for 1990 to 2000 data and http://eire.census.gov/popest/archives/1980.php for 1980 to 1990 data).

References & Data Sources

References

Arman, F., D. Samida, and M. Walker (1999). *Provincial Economic Freedom in Canada, 1981-1998*. Critical Issues Bulletin (January). Vancouver, BC: The Fraser Institute.

Barro, Robert, and Xavier Sala-i-Martin (1995). *Economic Growth*. New York: McGraw-Hill.

De Haan, Jakob, and Jan Egbert Sturm (2000). On the Relationship between Economic Freedom and Economic Growth. *European Journal of Political Economy* 16: 215–41.

Easton, Stephen, and Michael Walker (1997). Income, Growth, and Economic Freedom. *The American Economic Review* 87, 2: 328–32.

Gwartney, James, and Robert Lawson, with Walter Park and Charles Skipton (2001). *Economic Freedom of the World: 2001 Annual Report*. Vancouver, BC: The Fraser Institute.

Gwartney, James, and Robert Lawson. with Walter Park, Smita Wagh, Chris Edwards, and Veronique de Rugy (2002). *Economic Freedom of the World: 2002 Annual Report*. Vancouver, BC: The Fraser Institute, 2002.

Gwartney, J., R. Lawson, and W. Block (1996). *Economic Freedom of the World, 1975–1995*. Vancouver, BC: The Fraser Institute.

Knox, Robert (2002). Competitiveness Begins at Home. *Fraser Forum* (March): 15–16.

Mankiw, N. Gregory, David Romer, and David N. Weil (1992). A Contribution to the Empirics of Economic Growth. *Quarterly Journal of Economics* 107 (May): 407–37.

McMahon, Fred (2000a). *Retreat from Growth: Atlantic Canada and the Negative Sum Economy*. Halifax, NS: Atlantic Institute for Market Studies.

McMahon, Fred (2000b). *Road to Growth: How Lagging Economies Become Prosperous*. Halifax, NS: Atlantic Institute for Market Studies.

Data Sources

Advisory Commission on Intergovernmental Relations (1994). *Significant Features of Fiscal Federalism*. http://www.library.unt.edu/gpo/acir .

Antweiller, Werner (2001). Pacific Exchange Rate Service. University of British Columbia (as of December 2001). Retrieval form found at http://pacific.commerce.ubc.ca/xr/.

Arman, Faisal (1999). Occupational licensing information collected from provincial statute books. Published in *Provincial Economic Freedom, 1981-1998*, The Fraser Institute, 1999.

Bureau of Economic Analysis. United States Dep't of Commerce (http://www.bea.doc.gov as of December 2001).

Bureau of Labour Statistics, US Department of Labor (ftp://ftp.bls.gov/pub/special.requests/cpi/cpiai.txt, as of December 2001.

Bureau of Labour Statistics, US Department of Labor. *Monthly Labour Review* (various issues) (http://www.bls.gov/opub/mlr/mlrhome.htm).

Canadian Tax Foundation (various issues). *Finances of the Nation*.

Council of State Governments and the American Legislators' Association. *The Book of the States* (various issues). Chicago, IL.

Evans, R.G., and W.T. Stanbury (1980). *Occupational Regulation in Canada, a Background Study Prepared for the Economic Council of Canada, Regulation Reference*.

Federation of Tax Administrators. Available at http://www.taxadmin.org.

Financial Management System, Public Institutions Division, Statistics Canada (2001).

Human Resources Development Canada (December 2001) (http://206.191.16.130/psait_spila/lmnec_eslc/eslc/salaire_minwage/report2/report2_e.cfm).

Internal Revenue Service, Department of the Treasury. Available at http://www.irs.gov/.

National Center for Education Statistics, US Department of Education (December 2001) (http://nces.ed.gov/quicktables).

National Center for Education Statistics, US Department of Education (various issues). *Private High School Survey*.

Population Division, US Census Bureau, United States Department of Commerce (http://eire.census.gov/popest/archives) .

Smith-Peters, Lise, ed. (1994). *The Directory of Professional and Occupational Regulation in the United States and Canada*. The Council on Licensure, Enforcement and Regulation.

Statistics Canada. CANSIM (Label numbers D985116, D985398, D985680, D985962, D986244, D986526, D986808, D987090, D987372, and D987654).

Statistics Canada. CANSIM (Table 380-0056).

Statistics Canada. *Education*. Catalogue #81-229.

Statistics Canada (1981–2001). *Provincial Economic Accounts*.

The Tax Foundation (various issues). *Facts and Figures on Government Finances*.

US Census Bureau, US Department of Commerce (http://www.census.gov/govs/www/estimate.html; ftp://ftp.census.gov/pub/outgoing/; as of December 2001).

US Census Bureau, US Department of Commerce (various issues). *Consolidated Federal Funds Reports*.

US Census Bureau, US Department of Commerce (various issues). *Statistical Abstract of United States*.